INTO AFRICA

When you are upside-down, shoot from the roots

Cecile De Neuilly-Rice

authorHOUSE®

AuthorHouse™ UK Ltd.
500 Avebury Boulevard
Central Milton Keynes, MK9 2BE
www.authorhouse.co.uk
Phone: 08001974150

© *2010 Cecile De Neuilly-Rice. All rights reserved.*

No part of this book may be reproduced, stored in a retrieval system, or transmitted by any means without the written permission of the author.

First published by AuthorHouse 1/25/2010

ISBN: 978-1-4490-5385-7 (sc)

This book is printed on acid-free paper.

FOREWORD

No tree in Africa embodies the spirit of Africa more than the Baobab. It is known as the Tree of Life and also as the Upside-Down tree. It is an ancient tree, the oldest being 3000 years, and is capable of providing water, food, and shelter to animals and humans. Its many medicinal properties include a treatment for malaria and fever.

African legend has it that each animal was given a tree to plant and the hyena accidentally planted his tree upside-down. In some African cultures it is believed that, if you picked its flowers, a lion would eat you.

In the winter the Baobab looks upside-down. The stark naked, twisted branches seem like gnarled roots exposed to the mercy of the elements. What should be hidden and grounded, are now vulnerable and fair game for the vultures out there.

Life also turns us upside down at times. Hurts are exposed and we either try our best to hide and cover them up, surrender to our circumstances, or we decide to blossom and shoot new growth from the very source of our pain and vulnerability.

This is a journey through the heart of life: a story of adventure, fun and laughter, challenges, determination and victory.

The Baobab

When you feel you're going to drown
Feet up and head down
Remember the Baobab
In the winter so sad
Upside-down, naked and cold
But in truth, standing bold

With calculated patience

Drawing life from its roots
Carefully forming new shoots
Deep inside the womb
To blossom till long after the tomb
Leaving a legacy of love
Pure as snow, a gentle dove
Flying free on the wings of grace
Launched from The Rock, its base

For Clinton

Contents

Chapter 1.	Autumn 1987	1
Chapter 2.	The Baron Has Landed	5
Chapter 3.	Botswana	17
Chapter 4.	The Dust Settles	22
Chapter 5.	Rattletrap And The River	27
Chapter 6.	The Crossing	36
Chapter 7.	A Flying Jacana	47
Chapter 8.	Coming Home From Home	53
Chapter 9.	Operation Third World	60
Chapter 10.	Boomboo's First Visit	64
Chapter 11.	Murder On The River	68
Chapter 12.	A Close Encounter Of The African Kind	71
Chapter 13.	A Long Awaited Inspection	76
Chapter 14.	Kalahari Cascanades	79
Chapter 15.	A Miracle And Kubu	84
Chapter 16.	Deliverance	97
Chapter 17.	The Covenant	103
Chapter 18.	A Bright New Dawn	108
Chapter 19.	Kariba	112
Chapter 20.	Petals And Pleats	133
Chapter 21.	Free From Fear	139
Chapter 22.	Turning South	144
Chapter 23.	Tuli Block Days	149
Chapter 24.	My Dad. My Mentor	160
Chapter 25.	Ostrich Smuggling	162
Chapter 26.	The Land Of Canaan	167
Chapter 27.	The Return Of The Native	183
Chapter 28.	The Full Circle	191
Chapter 29.	A Cedar Falls	214
Chapter 30.	The Wedding	226

CHAPTER 1
AUTUMN 1987

I slept uneasily, perpetually scanning the walls and roof with the semi-exhausted torch beam for spiders. I hate these evil-looking, hairy creatures that seem to lurk in every fissure, appearing when least expected. They epitomized my fear of the unknown.

What am I doing here, for goodness' sake! Had I come to a life from the Dark Ages, a life of my ancestors, the Voortrekkers? The reality of my surroundings coldly pushed aside my dreams of raising my children in a comfortable and safe home with soft carpets and gentle touches.

Instinctively I reached for Clinton who was breathing rhythmically and peacefully next to me. I drew comfort and strength from his presence. As I gazed at his strong body and handsome face, I knew why I was here. I would follow this man to the ends of the earth.

My twenty-one month old daughter, Gisèle, and month old son Michael, were blissfully unaware of the turmoil inside me as they were sleeping, undisturbed by the dangers of our new environment; the bush in the heart of Africa.

For a girl accustomed to civilization, snakes, scorpions, spiders and hyenas on her doorstep represented very real dangers. But there was no time to dwell on dangers alone. There was a life to be lived, a new home to be made, children and a husband who needed care and attention. Above all, there was this incredible challenge to make a success of this new venture we had willingly chosen.

Our dwelling was a three roomed block-brick construction with a leaking asbestos roof, no ceilings, few unbroken window panes, rough cement floors, no secure doors and surrounded by dry wild grasses and acacias which harboured many a venomous snake. During the months Clinton had spent here preparing for our arrival, an Egyptian spitting cobra paid him a visit one night. He was sleeping on a mattress on the floor when his nocturnal visitor surprised him. No need to say who was airborne and out of the room first! Thank God he turned to look somewhere else when the cobra spat at him. The venom can blind a person for a while, so his relief was great when he wiped the trickle from his cheek.

We came to Botswana, enthusiastic entrepreneurs of a farming enterprise. Clinton and his brother Marc owned an irrigation business in Cradock, South Africa. The South African economy was severely strained by sanctions and ever-increasing political turmoil because of the government's policy of apartheid. They closed the business down and we chose to come to Botswana, the Switzerland of Africa, to start a new life. The pioneering spirit was in us and the challenge was upon us.

Financially we could not afford this move. After many in depth feasibility studies and a visit to Botswana, Carl van Lingen, a young farmer from the Middelburg (Cape) district, decided to back Clinton. They formed a company called Diranga Irrigation. Diranga is a Mbukushu word meaning good and strong. It is also the name of the area near Shakawe in the far North Western Botswana, where they had been granted six hundred hectares of prime land by the Ngami Land Board. The plan was to grow maize under several center pivots with water from the great Okavango River, the third mightiest river in Southern Africa. The Botswana government was very keen for farmers to grow maize on a scale like this and promises of subsidies and assistance were promptly made. However, Green Peace, backed by considerable international clout, decided that an irrigation scheme of this magnitude should not be allowed from the Okavango River, lest the Okavango Swamps be pumped dry! The Okavango rises in the western highlands of Angola within a few hundred kilometers of the Atlantic Ocean and plunging rapidly eastwards, it snakes out across the northern fringes of the Kalahari for more than a thousand kilometers to drop swiftly through the Popa Rapids and enters Botswana at Mohembo.

At this time the Botswana Government was also receiving reports of irregularities regarding land allocations in Ngamiland. Because of these factors, all recently approved projects in this area were frozen indefinitely. This was a severe blow to our plans, not to mention our budget. All our equipment had already been moved up this great distance from the Karoo at no small cost, the cut lines of the farm had been cleared and Clinton had started de-bushing. However, we were still committed to investing in Botswana because of various reasons.

Botswana is a fast developing Third World Country with a stable government boasting the fastest growing economy in Africa. Free enterprise is encouraged and operates on the sound basis of supply and demand. The demand is great for locally produced fresh food and the supply is just about non-existent. So we saw an opportunity we believed worth trying. The country's largest source of foreign exchange comes from its very high quality diamonds mined at Jwaneng and Orapa. Rich deposits of copper are smeltered in Selebi-Phikwe. Beef exported to the EEC is the next biggest earner of foreign exchange.

Because of the insistence by Green Peace, our project was put on hold. Our lawyer in Gaborone, the capitol of Botswana, put us in contact with Sekgoma Khama, the nephew of Sir Seretse Khama, who owned land lying waste in Selebi-Phikwe. Mr Khama saw the opportunity and agreed to lease the land to Diranga Irrigation in exchange for a share in the company. This was agreed to and we landed up in the Eastern part of Botswana.

Our great adventure had started. Little did we realize what this would entail. We could not conceive the privations, hardships and problems that would come to try us. Nor could we anticipate the upliftment with nature, nor the pristine joy that would be ours.

CHAPTER 2
THE BARON HAS LANDED

Our son, Michael, was born in Cape Town on 14 April 1987. Due to complications during my pregnancy, my gyneacologist advised me not to join my husband in the bush until after the birth. As a result, I spent six months in Bredasdorp at my parents' home. During this time I was pampered and spoilt and the transition from civilization to bush was more traumatic than I could ever imagine.

Clinton came to fetch us with the Baron, a twin-engine light aircraft, when Michael was three weeks old. I was elated at the prospect of being reunited with my husband and having my family together again, but I was headed for the unknown with a toddler and an infant and I was frightened! Could I cope in this new far away country? Could I survive the primitive lifestyle in the bush? I have always disliked dust and was no camper. I pretended to be brave and capable for my parents' sake. They were worried sick about this venture of ours and hardly disguised their apprehension. Because of my insecurity and confusion, it took an unprecedented effort on my part to keep my conflicting emotions from tearing me apart.

As always, my fears disappeared momentarily when Clinton held me tight and I melted against the warmth of his love. This man was ready for adventure and determined to overcome every obstacle to prove his loyalty and devotion to his family. I was hopelessly in love with him and being together under any circumstances was more comforting than anything else life could offer.

My parents drove us down to the small landing strip on the outskirts of Bredasdorp in silence. I wanted to sound cheerful and positive, but found I couldn't trust my voice. I just wanted to make the parting as painless as possible for them. In spite of the greatest effort to put on a brave face, I was unable to stop the painful stinging of tears as I looked into my Dad's eyes.

Little Gisèle had grown very close to my parents and her cousins. Apart from Michael, she was the youngest grandchild as well as the center of attraction. At the age of 21 months she had a large vocabulary and amazed us all by her independence. With Gisèle on his lap, Oupa (grandpa) had many conversations with her and she loved him to bits. He had the patience of Job with her and was rewarded with her devotion and loyalty. Nobody was allowed to say Oupa drove too slowly or that he could be difficult at times!

Oupa had a special drawer in his cupboard where he kept a selection of his grandchildren's favourite sweets. This cupboard was always approached with a great deal of excitement as it unparsimoniously parted with its delicious contents at the slightest request from a grandchild. Oupa was often reprimanded for feeding the children sweets before a meal, but he would simply say that it was not his fault if the kids were hungry and the meal late! He often ignored an objection and would simply walk to the cupboard with Gisèle and André, my brother's youngest, following stealthily, always to emerge giggling conspiratorially. A trip down to the local store with Oupa was an adventure. Replenishments for the sweets drawer always ended with Oupa having to cut back on the requests for specific favourites as the bag became too heavy to carry!

Life in this beautiful little town was organized and relaxed. Whenever I needed an extra little nap in the afternoons to strengthen myself for the interrupted sleep at night, my mom would look after the children. She was also invaluable at night when the baby woke up. She would patiently burp and dry him after a feed to bless me with extra rest. She is one of the most unselfish people I know, always ready to give of herself and never too tired to serve others.

Gisèle formed a strong bond with Joanie, my brother's only daughter, despite the five-year age gap between them. Joanie mothered her and entertained her with her bubbling good nature and kindness. Kobus, the eldest of the three, often found himself on all fours with Gisèle riding horse on his back. To this day, these cousins are very close. On that sad morning the parting was all the more distressing because of this close bond.

Before we boarded the Baron, the silence between us became quite pronounced. Gisèle, being so young, was caught up in the excitement of our imminent flight. The revving engines mercifully drowned out a couple of sobs from the other children and served as a distraction from the anguish of our departure. However, when Oupa gently folded Gisèle's little fingers over a packet of her favourite sweets, we all wept unashamedly. Clinton realized it was time to take off and soon we were airborne to our uncertain future. I looked down at the small waiving group with blurred vision. My known, safe and caring world slowly disappeared and I reeled with apprehension.

Two hours later we landed at Twistkraal, Carl's farm in the Karoo. We spent two days there and then flew to Pretoria from where we continued our journey to Botswana in a thirty-ton truck and trailer that carried all our earthly possessions.

We left Pretoria at noon on Thursday and arrived at Martin's Drift Border Control Post at half past five in the afternoon. The trip thus far had been hot and tiring. Michael's routine was disturbed and he became niggly. The heat was oppressive as we travelled north and this did nothing to endear me to Botswana. After all the formalities at the border post we continued to our first stop at Roy and Charlotte Young's ranch in the Tuli Block, approximately sixty kilometers inland. Twenty kilometers before their ranch, Botswana's terrible dirt roads dealt me my first taste of hardship in the bush. We had a punctured tyre and were forced to stop. I always thought a country's roads were a fair indication of the level of its civilization. I felt a distinct disdain towards Botswana as our host country. The bush on either side stretched out mournful and supplicating branches, as patiently all nature awaited the infrequent, longed for rains of the coming season.

The warm twilight folded its dusty arms around the area we were stranded. Thirsty mosquitoes started circling and I was tired and miserable. Michael, who had been shaken up for seven hours due to the vibrations of the truck, was now exercising his lungs at full volume, telling the world he had had enough. Thank God he was breastfed and I plugged him in to calm him down.

Clinton was trying to change the huge tyre, but needed help. He called to me and I stubbornly refused to leave my baby to the mercy of the malaria carrying mosquitoes. I was so disenchanted with my lot that I shouted back at him warning him I would use the wheel spanner on him instead. His only assistance came from Gisèle who was never too tired to help her favourite man. She slid down the side of the cab and landed with a thud in the powdery dust. Looking up at me I saw tears on her cheeks looking like little rivulets in a dry and dusty landscape. I didn't know whether to cry or curse. But she was on a mission to help her dad. The sight of Gisèle hanging on the wheel spanner must have given Clinton the power he needed to do the job by himself. Back in the cab a little tender loving care quickly made her smile again and all was well, except that she looked like an orphaned bush baby covered in dust. Needless to say Clinton was upset that I wouldn't help him.

When we eventually arrived at the Young's ranch, my only desire was for a warm bath where I could soak away my worries. Charlotte was charming and kind. She grew up in the Southern Cape and we had much in common. She ran a bath for the children and I was rewarded with a first smile from Michael. All seemed normal as the kids were enjoying the comforting and familiar soak in the tub, until Gisèle decided it would be good to add more oil to the water. The bottle slipped and its entire contents were emptied into the bath. I could scarcely hold on to my baby's slippery little body and Gisèle lost her footing, creating a wave of oily water all over the floor. Now my footing was compromised and I had to get both out of the bath quickly. I couldn't decide which was worse – the dust or the oil.

Matters were hardly improved when Roy asked me if I had any idea of what my future home looked like. Roy and Charlotte had been there a couple of weeks before and when I replied that I had no idea, he regarded me sympathetically and just shook his head. This was not good and I felt panic creeping up on me. Surely these good people would have been a little more positive if there had been any reason to be. My pride would not let me admit defeat, but my heart grew faint at the thought of tomorrow. The rest of the evening I spent fighting off mosquitoes and in doing so ensured no one else got much sleep either.

The night seemed endless and my thoughts became more dysfunctional as the hours passed. Deep inside me doubt and fear started breeding and gave birth to its offspring of resentment, anger and self-pity. My anchor of comfort and predictability had been hoisted from its deep waters of parental care and familiarity. This burden was threatening to sink my now wobbly little ship.

The last leg of our journey took two hours. When, at last, we arrived in Selebi-Phikwe, I tried to get a reasonable view of the town, but we were on a bypass and my first impression was vague. What I did see was not very inspiring, but with daylight came a renewed sense of hope and I refused to be too disheartened. We travelled on for another hour through mopani bush and had to ford the dry Motloutse river bed before we came to a shack about a hundred meters from the dry river. I glanced at Clinton in utter disbelief. "Dear Lord" I prayed religiously, "I really need Your help to stay composed."

When I saw Clinton's pleading look, I decided there and then – come hell or high water, I am going to make it! This place won't get me down. Together we'll meet this challenge, no matter what it takes. I managed a bewildered little smile and climbed out of the truck. I politely greeted the workers who approached their new "mother" enthusiastically. I closed my eyes for a moment, thinking, "This is Friday. Just take it one day at a time". When I opened my eyes a big black woman with a flashing smile and outstretched arms demanded my precious cargo. I clutched my baby tight, refusing to hand him over until Clinton introduced Gobopamang, our new housekeeper.

"Dumela Mma," she greeted me in a gentle voice. She obviously sensed my distrust and kept her distance. She was genuine in her welcome, but I still reluctantly handed over my baby, keeping Gobopamang near me all the time. I only relaxed a little when I saw how protectively she held him. Michael would become very fond of his Gogemang, as he later called her.

My gaze swept the territory and I realized that this challenge was indeed a great one. The khaya (shack) in front of me had been white washed in a hurry to lend a dismal air of respectability to it. The primitive world around me was completely foreign to me. I could hear the hideous laughter of the bush mocking my inability to cope, daring me to run before I unpacked, pre-concluding my defeat. I stood transfixed before I was able to speak.

Constance, one of the women who helped around the house, called us for a cup of tea she had prepared. Her four-year-old daughter waited behind a tree to play with Gisèle. I was grateful for a friend for Gisèle even if they could not understand each other's language yet. I struggled to organize our khaya into some kind of habitable dwelling for the night. Michael was demand-fed and demanded his feed every three hours, day and night. I was worn down and started losing weight fast.

All my belongings were still packed away in boxes. Trying to run a household in this chaos was very difficult. There simply was no space in this little pondok (shack) to fit in a quarter of my furniture. There were no shelves, no cupboards, only ugly space contained by bare walls. The ever-present fine powdery dust continually settled on everything, driving me mad. I decided that my first priority would be a lawn around the shack to minimize the dust. It proved to be easier living out of boxes, rather than unpack stuff that had to be washed before you could use it anyway.

Gisèle had to be scrubbed down before every meal. She loved cavorting outside in the dirt. Cleaning under her nails was quite a performance and always ended up in a screaming match. It was impossible to maintain any decent form of hygiene under those circumstances. Sometimes I would stare out over the landscape and long for the rolling green wheat lands of the Overberg. My nostalgia did not help my mood and I had to speak to myself harshly.

This was a fight for survival and I would have to adapt or die. I tried to find beauty in the things around me and realized the camel thorn trees surrounding us were in fact attractive, provided they kept their thorns on themselves. I learnt to distinguish between venomous and non-poisonous snakes. We had moved into their previously undisturbed territory and they were putting up a good fight. I often had to shoot a cobra or shield-nose in the yard. The staff wanted to kill every snake they saw and I had to convince them some were harmless and should be allowed to live. They never fancied this theory and thought I was quite mad.

Our cooking was done on an outside open fire. Water was carried from the river and heated in a big black three-legged cast iron pot. There was no water on tap, no electricity, no telephone, no nothing. Washing was done by hand and ironing with an ancient appliance that cocked open to reveal a cavity for hot coals. Our clothes had to be ironed because of putsi flies that laid their eggs in damp surfaces. These eggs would hatch into worms under your skin creating an infected, itchy area. The only way to get rid of them was to wait for a day or two and them squeeze them out. The hole left behind would then have to be disinfected and the scar would disappear with time. The poor animals that rolled in any damp surface were inundated with putsies.

Two days after our arrival six South African friends on a hunting trip arrived for Sunday lunch. I hadn't even unpacked our cutlery or crockery. I was frantic! Pat Cawood and her hunting party from Maun were much better organized. I was still scurrying around trying to find enough plates when she offloaded her trunk containing crystal glasses and superior Cape wine. Pat did everything in style. Thanks to inebriation no one took much notice of the food. I gave up on etiquette and joined the raucous party.

Pat Cawood was the first South African woman to be registered as a professional hunter. She had lost her husband, Mike, in a tragic explosion on their farm a year before and was carrying on with Mike's hunting business in Botswana. Southern Cross Safaris had a good name internationally and Pat made sure that didn't change. Apart from her good looks, she had heaps of energy and drive. A very capable lady indeed.

Into Africa

We forgot about our primitive surroundings as we sipped KWV Roodeberg from Pat's crystal glasses in the shade of the old camel thorn. I thought of the great distance between the bush and my beloved Cape of Good Hope.

I was faced with another dilemma. Where would I put them to sleep? There were three rooms – a bedroom, a kitchen/lounge, and a storeroom with one bed and no door. Between the Land Cruiser and the storeroom everyone managed to find a spot. When they left the following day, all the glamour vanished too.

"Clinton having a bath"

"Gisèle and Michael in shower"

Going off in the pick-up to find a secluded spot in the veld for ablutions became something of the past when, after a month, Clinton completed the "bathroom". A shower, basin and a flush toilet with a drain under the tank stand seemed very grand compared to the bush and tin bath. This bathroom was enclosed with reeds and had no roof. The water tank was directly above so the pressure in the shower was great. I was so grateful for this improvement. Hot water came from a 44-gallon drum heated by a fire just outside the enclosure. Things I had taken for granted, like a bathroom, now birthed such gratitude. The bush had certainly humbled me. The joy this luxury brought could not be outdone by a bottle of French perfume or a diamond ring. I was even appreciative of the moon and stars shining down on me under the shower while the delicious water cleansed my soul and body. The children were too small to shower, so I put the faithful old sink tub in the shower, filled it from the shower and bathed them there. A visit to the toilet at night was always a little frightening because of the presence of spiders and scorpions. This little bathroom was built about ten meters outside the house.

One day, Gisèle and her little Motswana friend found two empty boxes that they converted into their vehicles. Gisèle was driving her car with a great deal of brrr.….ing and hooting and Catherine was beating her donkeys in front of her cart. As I watched them fondly, their little game was depicting their respective backgrounds so accurately that I couldn't help laughing. Little did I know Michael, twenty months later, would sit on his rocking horse and also beat the "donkey's" bum with a stick!

I sat under the camel thorn tree and wrote my first letter to my parents. The days were sunny and the birds were chirping gaily. There was a certain primitive peace in the bush that seemed to slowly ease away my fears and doubts. In spite of myself, I experienced a sense of belonging and slowly conquered the culture shock that had so rudely rocked my world. I tried to soften the truth of our environment in my letter, partly because I didn't want my parents to pity me or think that Clinton was subjecting us to too much. They had very clearly defined conceptions of the role of a husband and father. Clinton was to be the provider and protector and I had to maintain the loving core of the family or "set the tone" as my mother would say. I agree wholeheartedly, but when survival is at stake, the roles overlap and both partners have to draw the cart side by side. I adapted to my role of fellow carthorse and found myself shooting snakes and crop-raiding monkeys, driving the tractor and being general farm manager when Clinton was away on business.

My circumstances changed my priorities and my general expectation of life. My father often said that truly great people never look down on others. Greatness is a quality of the heart, not the size of a wallet. He also said that a person must never deny his own heritage, people or background if he wants to keep the respect of others. I come from Afrikaans stock and was sent to an English school in Cape Town not to become English, but to learn the language and realize that people are basically the same. Every human being wants to be loved and love in return. We need human contact, kindness and appreciation. We also need to give the same. What makes me sad will make others sad. What you sow you will reap. He often used to say that if a person is armed with integrity and kindness, and have God on your side, nothing serious could go wrong. I am blessed to have grown up in a very close family.

My world had been one of comfort and self-centeredness. The bush was to educate me differently rather quickly.

CHAPTER 3
BOTSWANA

Our ground lay between the Letlhekane and Motloutse Rivers, fifteen kilometers outside Selebi-Phikwe. Tribal Trust Land cannot be bought as it belongs to all the people of Botswana. This land was allocated to Sekghoma Khama and we had a lease agreement with him for twenty years, with an option to renew this lease. The famous Sir Seretse Khama was his uncle and his own father, Tsekhedi Khama, was the regent of Botswana during the time of Seretse's exile to England.

Seretse Khama was educated in England and met Ruth Williams while he was still a student. They fell in love and wanted to get married. There were, however, enormous complications due to the fact that she was a white girl from another country and he was a black paramount chief from Africa. In those days the race issue posed problems for both of them. The elders in Botswana did not want their leader to marry outside his culture and a kghotla gathering was called to discuss this dilemma. Seretse brought her to meet his people. Eventually they received the blessing of the Batswana, but met with enormous opposition from their neighbouring country, South Africa. The apartheid regime in South Africa saw this marriage as a threat to stability in their country because of its racial policy of apartheid. Eventually pressure from England and South Africa forced the couple into exile. It took courage and a long time for this issue to be resolved, but eventually they returned to Botswana to lead their country to prosperity and stability.

Sekghoma had become our friend. He is a gentleman and very well educated. Socializing with a black person on this level was novel for us. We found it easy to talk and laugh together. It was a liberating experience that taught me some important lessons in life. I recall hearing his beautiful tenor voice ringing out from the shower under the tank stand one morning. He had brought his son, who was at school in Zimbabwe, to visit us. After a most enjoyable time we were sad to say good-bye to both of them.

The climate in Botswana is one of extremes. On a hot summers day the mercury would rise to 47º C and drop to 36º C at night. In the winter months the days could be warm, but the nights were bitterly cold. In our first year I felt like a wilted spinach leaf most of the time. I actually thought it was possible to suffer brain damage in this heat. One day Gaborone was the hottest recorded city in the world at 53º C. My children kept on stripping off their clothes in an attempt to cool down. The merciless African sun bronzed us and left me with two sweaty, dusty and very dirty kids at the end of each day. We slept under mosquito nets at night, which did not help the cooling off process.

Malaria was not too common in our area, but after the rains there were some recorded cases. Botswana medical advice was not to take malaria tablets, as the prolonged usage of the drug could cause all sorts of health problems. These drugs would often suppress the symptoms of malaria and this in itself posed a problem. Malaria had to be treated very quickly. Many visitors to Botswana who contracted malaria would be diagnosed back home as suffering from influenza.

Time is not of the essence in this country. Patience, if not inbred, had to be acquired to keep sanity at an acceptable level. I marveled at the natural patience of the locals. Waiting in queues was a given. These times were used to catch up on local gossip and other news. Queuing and waiting was an acceptable social pass time often interspersed with entertainment on site. People in queues spoke loudly so that no one could accuse them of slander or malicious gossip.

The Batswana women dress smartly and wear good shoes. They are always clean and neat. Hats, because of the sun, were in vogue, always displaying the intricate plaits of extensions in the hair. Older women never wore trousers, especially married ladies. Adult men would not be seen dead in shorts. Traditional dress was a little outdated in Gaborone, the only large city in Botswana, but in the bush it was the order of the day. A woman who had not proven her fertility by bearing a child, found it hard for the man to marry her. Marriage was a serious matter and the whole family's blessing was required. The bridegroom's uncle would traditionally act as mediator between the two families in order for the ceremony to take place. Lobola, a traditional gift from the bridegroom to the bride's parents, was negotiated by the uncle as well. This would normally be paid in the form of cattle. A daughter was thus born as an asset to the family.

The system of Government was very interesting. Members of parliament were elected democratically where each constituency was represented by its own MP. A Westminster system of governance operated alongside the traditional tribal House of Chiefs. The House of Chiefs had no legislative power, but had great influence. Bills were presented to this body for approval before new laws were passed. In this way the nation was kept happy and informed. Local matters were addressed by the chief at his kghotla gatherings. This is a meeting of the elders of the community, as well as any other member of the community, who will hold court and pass judgment on offenders of petty theft, personal quarrels, grazing disputes and all other general complaints. The tribal police could imprison offenders after sentence was passed by the chief. If the verdict was caning, it was done immediately and in public. This was a great humiliation to the offender who would have lost respect in the community. Batswana are generally more afraid of Kghotla justice because of the shame brought to the family name.

The chief is usually chosen from members of the royal families. The youngsters are closely watched by the elders, who later decide on the strongest leader. This young man is then trained by the elders for his future duties.

When a married woman's husband dies, the eldest brother-in-law becomes head of her family and takes care of them. He also has the right to father children with her if she is still of child bearing age. If she should want to marry any other man, she needs consent from her brother-in-law. This second husband then pays lobola to him.

First time brides accept parental authority and guidance without question. If the chosen bridegroom is not the love of her life, she learns to love and obey him. When a mother dies, the eldest daughter becomes the mother and her sisters will then address her as mother. The matriarch stays at home to take care of the children while the younger mothers find jobs to help support the family.

Men basically delegate work to the women who tend the lands and animals. Today many men work on the mines or elsewhere to bring in money.

Most of these families live on cattle posts; thatched huts built in close proximity to each other and enclosed by a wooden-pole fence. Inside this enclosure the ground is swept and kept free of grass. Snakes are disliked intensely.

At the moment the ruling party is the Democratic Party, supported by the vast majority of Bamangwato (the largest tribe in Botswana). Their success in building up their country is founded on their wisdom to embrace both the traditional and the western cultures. The man in the street and the man on the cattle post are considered and respected.

The people of Botswana are peace loving and more interested in developing their own country than fighting futile wars. Botswana has truly become the Switzerland of Africa and attracts foreign investors with their open plan fiscal policies. Crime is minimal and co-operation is encouraged.

We loved the justice system, the people and the adventure. The climate, the red tape and roads were our only real challenges.

CHAPTER 4
THE DUST SETTLES

Inside our bedroom a fat gecko was a welcome guest, because it kept a respectable distance and earned its keep by catching mosquitoes, flies, moths and spiders. It was easy to watch it stalk its prey into the cracks between the roof and the walls. At night its activities provided great entertainment. As we cheered it on to capture its quarry, we became spectators to a fascinating game. We didn't have electricity, therefore no TV, but we did not want to exchange a live show for some far away TV performance. Our little acrobat was so quick in the attack and so adept at stuffing a huge meal into its tiny mouth, that Gisèle just loved its endless shows. We became fond of this little creature and eagerly anticipated its every move.

Wasps like making their nests inside protected areas, like our "holy" house where they have free access through all the gaps in the structure.

"Look! Mummy look!" Gisèle was pointing to a female wasp building a nest in the corner of the bookshelf. The wasp was too busy spitting out wet mud and smoothing it over to shape its nest to worry about its audience. The books merely gathered dust, but nature provided a live education to a fascinated learner.

My relationship with the crawlies around me had slowly been enhanced by the gradual appreciation and understanding of the wonderful place each little creature occupied in ecology. I still resented their presence in my house, though. I felt they had the whole world out there in which to live and I only had my little shack. I would not disturb them in their residences and they should respect my space, too.

I missed my appliances less and gently started unwinding in the peace of the bush. Gobopamang taught me to take things slower and to be more patient. She often said that the Lekgoa (whites) had no peace because we wanted things done today that could wait for tomorrow. There seemed to be no urgency to get anything done among the Motswana people. They are the most relaxed nation in the world, much to our frustration most of the time.

The dry, dusty area surrounding our dwelling had to be addressed and I started digging over the soil and planting lawn and shrubs. Gardening proved to be an effective remedy against self-pity. What you sowed you would reap, and nature was so generous in its reward. It is so easy to feel hard done by and I have realized that the shortest route to unhappiness is feeling sorry for your self. Self-pity is the single most useless emotion there is. Its harvest is always depression and darkness that robs you of joy and gratitude.

Hettie and Gerhard Gouws lived about thirty kilometers down river from us on a small plot. They had a wholesale fruit and veggie business in town. Their home was one small room, with a cupboard as partition between their bedroom and their children's. Surrounding this room was a corrugated iron enclosure, which contained an outdoor kitchen and bathroom. When I bewailed my lot, Gerhard exploded. He reminded me that our khaya was a lot bigger and I that I should be grateful and not complain.

That blew me off my pedestal. My understanding of the theory of relativity was clarified completely. In comparison to many others, we had nothing, and also much more. The key here was gratitude. Gratitude for health, food to eat, a family to love no matter what the circumstances. Cry and you cry alone, laugh and the world laughs with you.

It was bitterly cold in their little enclosure, but our hearts warmed to one another and a new, lasting friendship had been born. We drew strength from one another, encouraged one another and generally had a jolly time. Hettie is a formidable woman in every sense and I was inspired and encouraged by her attitude. She is physically and emotionally tough. She is up to any challenge and will off-load a ten ton truck of cabbage by herself, if need be. She dresses well, is groomed, unspoiled, and always ready for a laugh or a fight. I think it is her sincerity and zest for life that drew her to me. She was a living example that a person could survive in this uncivilized region, and therefore she gave me hope and courage to persevere.

Having grown up in Botswana, she could speak Setswana fluently. She could flatter and curse equally well in this language and the indigenous population adored her. She once locked herself and an alleged thief in her office and literally whipped him into spilling the beans. A well-known woman once tried to hide a nectarine between her breasts and was chased out of the shop by a furious Hettie. Look, no one took her for a ride, but everyone witnessed of her generosity and kindness. My children loved her and our children became close friends.

Back at the khaya we still had no electricity or telephone, despite the fact that both lines passed us at a distance of half a kilometer. We tried everything to get a connection, but to no avail. Remember, this is Botswana and electricity in the bush was considered an unnecessary luxury. The power lines went to the Nata quarry from where gravel and sand were sent off to the copper smelter in Selebi-

Into Africa

Phikwe. All our phoning and telexes had to be done in town from the office of Phikwe Filling Station. The owners were Daan and Julia Pelser. Daan is a very big man who used to be exceptionally strong. He once picked up the rear end of his Toyota Cressida for his co-driver to change a punctured tyre! His hands, head and frame were enormous. Daan and Julia were very kind to us and welcomed us with open arms. I often stayed the night at their home in town when Clinton was away on business.

During these overnight stays little Gisèle would fall asleep on Daan's huge chest. A lion's skin on the floor, complete with its stuffed head attached, intrigued her and Daan told the most wonderful stories about its history. I think she believed he killed that lion bare handed! Both Gisèle and Michael often sat on the head and pretended they had just been on a safari. Their home became a haven of peace to me in my adaptation to the bush.

Julia had a collection of gardening books and I found new ideas for my ever- expanding garden. The local municipality had a large nursery where hardy plants and trees were sold very cheaply. I became a regular customer and my garden started taking shape. I absolutely loved planning new areas and the joy my first flowers brought me, was overwhelming. My passion for gardening was born in that arid, ugly bush where the elements were always against me. Clinton also loved the garden and made sure there was an irrigation line available for the garden most of the time. We irrigated the lands with the help of a diesel generator, which supplied electricity to the pump at the river. Because the water was sub-surface, a large pit had to be dug in the riverbed for water to siphon through before we could pump from the Lethelakane River.

I was fascinated by the creativity of landscaping and pictured my surroundings changing into an oasis of colour to buffer my soul against the dirt and dust. Unbeknown to me, this new passion would pave the way to my future career in landscaping.

We had settled down in the bush and slowly started making a new life for ourselves. My expectations of life had shifted dramatically. Every day brought along new challenges and new solutions. I realized I was a lot tougher than I thought, and ventured out with confidence, knowing I could create a happy home for my family, even here in the most unlikely of places.

Home is not only a place. It is where one feels protected, welcome, at ease and free to make mistakes without fearing rejection. It is, in a sense, an arena in which you are encouraged to experiment and test the waters while knowing a lifeboat is at hand in the case of an emergency.

My lifeboat had been the predictable. Here, surrounded by the unknown, I realized I would have to commission a better-suited vehicle to carry me on my journey forward.

CHAPTER 5
RATTLETRAP AND THE RIVER

Our khaya became our home. The garden expanded until the maize land and limited water supply curtailed its growth. I was absorbed in the wonder of nature and the resilience I discovered within myself. I was aware of the inner peace and happiness I was experiencing. Even little blessings were not taken for granted. Hardship had written its message of perseverance deep in my soul. Nobody enjoys the pain involved in the process of becoming fit, but everybody enjoys being fit.

My children loved life in the bush. Clinton and I were happy and optimistic about our future in our foster country. We deeply cherished the love we shared for each other. Our marriage had entered a deeper sphere and the joy in our relationship reflected this.

My family often asked me how I managed to accept this incredibly hard and different life. All I could say was that I had all the ingredients a person needed for happiness: a loving, if somewhat too adventurous, husband, happy and healthy children and a lovely garden!

A bone of contention was the condition of our vehicle and the road through the river to our farm. The river was dry most of the year and the crossing, at the confluence of two rivers, had to be made over the sand. This would not be a problem in a four-wheel dive, but up till then I had to drive a two-wheel-drive pick-up through this thick sand. I used to stop on the bank, scan the track for any humps, flatten these obstacles with my slip-slop (a flat sandal), girdle the children down so that they would not become air-borne, and proceed at just the correct speed to reach the opposite bank. I got stuck a couple of times and would then carry the children all the way home. I became quite good at driving in the sand and, on a couple of occasions, shamed experienced off-roaders to win a bet. Clinton had bought a very old four-wheel-drive Land Rover to ensure easier crossings. It was as gray as its track record. You could never tell when or where something under the bonnet would give up the ghost. One of our friends stuck a Boys' Scout badge that read "Be Prepared", on its grill, much to my amusement and Clinton's annoyance.

This rattletrap would never have been declared roadworthy in South Africa. On occasions it would throw open its left front door on rounding a bend. The brakes needed pumping before responding and the indicators were the driver's arms- a straight right arm for a right turn and a circular motion for a left turn. To keep control I would put Michael on my lap and breast-feed him to keep him still, Gisèle would stand behind my left shoulder where I could wedge her against the seat as this contraption was built before the days of seat belts.

To complicate matters, if it were possible, I lost the ignition key and then had to learn to start the vehicle without a key. This procedure was very embarrassing. I had to open the bonnet, create a short circuit between the solenoid and the battery cable with a screw driver while standing on the front bumper with my behind up in the air! I felt like an ostrich with its head in a hole, while being

Into Africa

overly conscious of the amazed stares from onlookers. Because of this un-ladylike posture, which became part of my everyday existence, I could only wear shorts or jeans or be arrested for indecent exposure.

After a polite conversation with a prominent lady outside the Post Office one day, I needed to get going, but cringed at the thought of her witnessing my bonnet ritual. She was in no hurry and lingered while I tried to casually slip the screwdriver into position without climbing on the bumper. Her curiosity got the better of her and she wanted to know if this was a regular problem. I became irritated with all the attention from her and other onlookers. Didn't she ever encounter car problems? Had she forgotten this was a third world country where everything didn't always work first time?

I pretended this was no problem and stuck the screwdriver into position casually, only to find myself letting out a scream as the blooming thing shocked the lights out of me. She thought I was being electrocuted and tried to separate me from the source with a mighty swing of her handbag against my head. I landed on the pavement at the feet of some incredulous spectators. To hell with my pride, which had been reduced to rubble, anyway, I thought and staggered to my feet, got on the bumper with my bum up in the air and started the skedonk the only possible way. I rushed off to Hettie's fruit and veg shop to lick my wounds over a cup of tea. I was furious, but only had myself to blame. The thought of attacking Clinton did cross my mind, but I knew he would laugh so heartily that I decided to scrap that idea.

Gouws Farming Enterprises is situated in a dirt square about seventy meters from the tarmac road. They import fresh fruit and vegetables from South Africa twice weekly. They brought in loads of cabbage, onions and tomatoes for the local population. Hettie also made sure she stocked other fancy foods like mushrooms and baby marrows for the ex-pats. She often packed a big box of all sorts for us and refused payment most of the time. Beef in

Botswana was relatively inexpensive. Beef fillets were the cheapest cuts at four pula each, the reason being that the locals preferred meat on a bone. We mostly bought fillet which we barbequed, cooked, roasted and stewed, much to the amazement of my family who thought a fillet curry was the height of indulgence.

Hettie and Gerhard's son, Renaldo, was a year older than Gisèle and never missed an opportunity to visit us on the farm. When I walked to the rattletrap I found him sitting next to Gisèle, ready with his little suitcase packed. Hettie gave him one look, shook her head and said, "Moef!", her pronunciation of move. When Hettie said moef, you moef! The two little friends looked at each other tearfully and her heart grew soft.

"Ag okay man, loop! Jy gaan net nie vanaand tjank vir my nie!" (Go, but you had better not cry for me tonight!). She grabbed some more food supplies from her shop and sent us packing. Renaldo had the widest smile and his little face couldn't hide his excitement at the prospect of spending another evening in the company of his dear friend.

En route we had to stop at the abattoir to collect wet cow hides Clinton was salting and drying for an overseas company who used the leather for patches on the Lee jeans. It was lunchtime and none of the workers were prepared to load them. I couldn't wait for another hour and decided to load them myself. The weight of a wet hide was astonishing. Every time I nearly got one on the truck, it would slip and tumble to the ground. Now I was fuming, but my anger gave me enough power to load three hides. I was covered in a bloody, slimy mess and smelled like cow dung. The kids just pinched their noses and picked up a few new adjectives. At home Clinton realized I had had a hard day when he saw the mess and the mood. I vowed I would not pick up another hide as long as I lived.

He decided it was safer to take the children for a drive to the ostriches and give me time to clean up and cool down. When I had showered and changed, he suggested a glass of wine on the lawn under the old camel thorn tree. I told him that we didn't have money for alcohol, to which he replied, "My Love, this is for medicinal purposes only." His sense of humour and his wicked little smile bowled me over, as always, and the two of us sat down to relax while the children played happily in the sand pit. After the second glass I started giggling at this new world of ours. We felt strangely at home, at peace and at ease. He took me in his arms and kissed away all my anger and frustration. My love for him made it impossible to stay angry. We watched the red sunset in silent content.

Going to town was an ordeal for me. It was so hot and two small, demanding children didn't make things easier. Michael had to go with because his milk supply was connected to me. Gisèle always loved the outing. The duration of our stay in town was determined by the length of the queues in the Post Office and at the bank. Batswana never did anything in a hurry. This was the single most frustrating characteristic of this peaceful nation. There was always time for a chat and gossip, no matter how urgent your business or short your time. Chris Biddulph, an ex bank manager from Zimbabwe turned businessman in Selebi-Phikwe, once lost it in the bank after queuing for an hour and a half. He deserted the queue, burst into the manager's office and hurled his bag of money at the docile gentleman trapped behind his desk.

"I've had enough! Now YOU will bank this money for me!", he shouted at the top of his voice. The missile had missed the manager's head by inches and he was so shocked that he agreed immediately. Chris was well known for his short fuse.

One of the most embarrassing incidents happened in the post office one morning. Gisèle had just been potty trained and was so proud of herself. She waited in the post office with her nanny for me to finish. From experience she knew that the wait would be long. When she couldn't hold out any longer, she dropped a turd right there on the floor. Anna, her nanny, was mortified and rushed out with her. On my way out I saw this nasty little package on the floor and was disgusted. Outside I mentioned this to Anna, who grabbed my arm and pulled me to the pick-up. I still had other chores to do nearby at the grocery shop, but Anna was adamant. We had to leave immediately and forget about further shopping. I was confused and demanded an explanation. Anna sank down low in her seat and told me to drive away quickly. After a minute or two she said that my child had messed in the Post Office and that she could not show her face there again, as she was sure on of the attendants had seen her rush out without cleaning up. I insisted on going back to clean up, but Anna said she would rather resign than face this ordeal. That settled it. Anna was worth more to me than an angry Post Office official. At home Clinton thought it was hilarious until he realized he would have to do the post office stops for a while, and Anna decided that we didn't share the same sense of humour.

One evening, as we were getting ready for bed, we heard someone shouting from somewhere in the bush. Clinton went out to investigate. Sure as nuts, a "Clinton!!" echoed from the opposite riverbank.

"Is that you Will?" Clinton shouted back.

"Yeah. How do we get to you people?"

"Stay where you are. I am coming to get you."

If you think I was dumbfounded by this faceless conversation, you should have heard the comments by William's girlfriend, Linda. The poor girl had never been to the bush before. William had asked her to take a trip with him to Botswana. She was working in Johannesburg at the time and William farms in the Murraysburg district in the Karoo.

She was appalled at the state of the road between Zanzibar border post and Selebi-Phikwe, a pot-holed, corrugated dirt road. By the time they arrived in Selebi-Phiwe it was almost dark, and she was so happy to see lights again. When William by-passed the town and headed towards the bush, she was up in arms. Couldn't they just overnight in town? William would have none of it and continued on this stretch of dirt that took them deeper into the darkness. When they came to a dead stop on the bank of a river in the middle of no-where, William got out of the vehicle and started shouting. Linda, tired and fed-up at this stage, thought Will had lost his marbles. She had had enough of the bush.

When, somewhere out of the pitch-black night, a voice answered him, she was amazed. She just shook her head in disbelief.

After supper, William filled the sink tub with hot water from the pot on the fire and carried it to their room for Linda to bathe her exhausted body. When we heard a few giggles from their room, we knew her amusement had overcome her initial shock at our way of life in the bush.

We were meeting people from all walks of life – beggars, wealthy town folk curious about our lifestyle, adventurers, hunters, good folk and crooks, communist mafia, and Taiwanese investors. The Botswana government, in an attempt to curb unemployment, had introduced a financial assistance plan whereby labour costs were heavily subsidized. This FAP policy encouraged various European investors to utilize the cheap labour in Botswana. Clothing factories, builders' warehouses and many more enterprises were built in the industrial area of town.

Our favourite was Robert Lee, a businessman with vested interests all over the globe. He used to travel with a huge entourage of guards and assistants. They always stayed at the Bosele Hotel in Selebi-Phikwe, but insisted on visiting us on the farm in the bush, much to the discomfort of his team. He needed leather for his overseas jeans company and had asked Clinton to organize the purchasing of bovine hides in Botswana.

His first visit caused a little commotion in our camp. We did not have a lounge or any decent facilities. We decided to carry out the sofa and chairs onto the lawn under the faithful old camel thorn tree. My lawn was an emerald carpet, and the setting sun had dressed the sky in burnt orange and red. Even the dry acacias on the horizon looked picture-perfect, clothed in dark silhouettes. The coffee table with its white cloth completed an elegant setting in the serenity of the evening. The only background music came from the birds singing their evensongs.

The previous day I had asked Clinton what kind of food I should prepare, not knowing Taiwanese customs. He said not to worry, he had asked his farm hands to prepare grilled mopani worms and sheba.

"They prefer insects and reptiles," he said, looking away to hide his smile.

I called his bluff and replied that I would then just serve them, seeing that women are not always welcome at Oriental dinners.

"Remember to dress the part – long dress, bare feet, quiet and efficient. The host will have you for desert."

We started laughing like naughty school kids.

"You do realize that most female insects eat the male after mating?" I said.

"Only when he is of no use to the female afterwards. In that case I am not worried."

Despite our fight for survival against the elements, we enjoyed the most wonderful life together. We made our own fun and laughter. Gisèle and Michael brought a new dimension to the fulfillment we enjoyed in our marriage. We stood united and because of our devotion to each other, we could face any obstacle in our way.

The grand party arrived. Our visitors fell in love with the setting – a haven of green in the middle of the arid bush. I was presented with a beautiful stone of white jade mounted in an ornate wooden carving and Clinton was given a case of Chivas Regal whiskey. We had a wonderful time with them, despite the fact that only Mr. Lee could speak English fluently. Robert Lee is a kind gentleman adept in western culture. And, before I forget, we had roast fillet and vegetables for dinner! After this visit, Mr. Lee always spent an evening with us during his one-day stopovers in Selebi-Phikwe. This annoyed the directors of Perfect Clothing Company who wanted to entertain and impress him at the Syringa Lodge in town.

I always enjoyed watching Clinton interacting with people. He never tried to impress people and never looked down on anyone. He simply enjoyed the conversation in his typical laid-back manner. His sense of humour was irresistible and his bellowing laughter broke down any barrier of unfamiliarity. He had a gift of putting people at ease and calming stormy waters. At the same time he almost always got his own way.

CHAPTER 6
THE CROSSING

It was unbearably hot and dry. During the day we gasped for air that seemed to singe our lungs. At night our beds burned our bodies. We were parched and drained all the time. I could not believe that the locals worked happily in this excruciating heat. I had obviously not acclimatized yet. Both human and beast yearned for the life giving, cooling drops of mercy from the heavens.

Clinton said that we'd all go to heaven, having had our hell on earth. In the evenings we would pull up our chairs next to the sprinklers irrigating the maize to catch a whiff of the cool spray. At bedtime we would empty a bucket of water over our mattress and sheets. After a couple of hours the bedding would be dry and the burning heat from the cement floors would reach up through the mattress to torture our exhausted bodies. My babies never needed diapers at night as they sweated out all excess fluids.

The first rains came in October and brought both relief and terror. We rushed to waterproof our shack with the enormous green tarpaulin we used to protect our move to Botswana on the truck. The tarpaulin covered our entire roof and stopped the rain gushing through the cracks in the asbestos sheets.

"Our Khaya"

Batswana don't work in the rain. All work stops as people stare at the tiny rivulets in the sand becoming great torrents cutting through the dusty landscape. The sound of thunder preceded the silent, dirty white foaming mass moving swiftly ahead of the rushing torrents. The usually dry and docile Motloutse and Lethlekane Rivers awoke from their slumber and turned into two hungry, angry serpents, devouring everything in their path, roaring and lashing out at saplings and stately old trees on the banks.

The transformation of the area was amazing. Almost overnight the dry barren land had come alive, cleansed of the thick layers of smothering dust. A course green blanket dotted with tiny yellow flowers covered the earth. The pale blue sky became azure, laden with the promise of more rain.

People everywhere became energized and started plowing and planting, proclaiming their new faith in nature. The birds' song was animated and echoed the happy chattering of the locals. All living things responded joyously to the rain.

This long awaited blessing brought along challenges of its own. Roads became muddy slip and slides. The rivers could not be crossed as they were in full flood. We were effectively cut off from town, except for a three-hour detour with the tractor. After ten days the raging torrent had subsided slightly and I had to get to town for supplies. The only way was in the huge 4x4 Mercedes tractor through a narrow section of the Lethlekane quite a way upstream.

This was daunting as I had my two children with me in the canopy. I remember staring at the fast flowing river ahead and wondering if the riverbed had been eroded away by the flood. There was no way I could tell and I slowly approached the crossing while using adjectives not usually found in my vocabulary. The brakes on the tractor were not very effective and I felt the merciless grip of fear slowly strangling me as we descended towards the water. Is the tractor high enough to cross the river without water flooding into the canopy and drowning us? Despite knowing Clinton had crossed there with this same tractor a day before, I still tensed up with fear as the murky waters started washing over the front tyres. There was no turning back as I felt the tractor sinking down into the river. My heart pounded so violently that I started shaking. The tractor's nose continued its descent into the water. Just as I was considering jumping ship, the nose slowly started rising and I felt a rush of gratitude and relief like I have never experienced before. Tears flowed freely as the tension broke. Shit! I exclaimed, and thought I was living in the wrong place at the wrong time and with the wrong attitude.

When I arrived in town I stopped at a friend's house. Pat Gold lived in luxury and once told me if I could live happily in that shack on the farm, she didn't need her psychiatrist any longer. Her car was at the garage for a service and I offered her a lift, which she accepted, until she saw my mode of transport outside her gate.

Her eyes widened in surprise and she just laughed. She could not be seen driving in a tractor in town!

After I had finished my chores, I headed home and the dreadful anticipation of crossing that river started clouding my mood. However, the water had subsided quite a lot and the crossing was a lot less stressful. I burst out laughing when I heard Gisèle saying, "Shit!" just as we were in the middle of the crossing. I told her to refrain from using that ugly word.

"Is it ugly, Mommy?" she asked innocently.

'Yes, my darling."

"Why, Mommy?"

"It just isn't a nice word to use."

"Oh." I could see the confusion in her expression and knew Clinton would be informed and interrogated.

Slowly, I had become a survivor and did not dwell on what I didn't have, but on the good things I did have. I tried not to think of the comforts I had left behind in South Africa, but brainwashed myself into believing this adventure was great fun most of the time.

On occasions I suffered nostalgic moments. I thought of my childhood and the carefree days of my youth. I remembered the first romantic thoughts I had on marriage and my future husband. I had it all sorted out. I would follow a brief, but successful career after I married the perfect man. Our children would grow up in a lovely home and have their mother with them all day and every day, because my husband would be wealthy enough to allow me to just be a mom at home. They would be brilliant sportsmen and distinguished academics. Our marriage would be filled with laughter, fun and ecstasy. Oh, how innocent and utterly immature I must have been to think that anyone would be spared hardships and trials. How presumptuous I was to believe that I deserved only the best. How shallow I was to not realize that you could only gain capacity through conquering pain and persevering through tough times. You only truly appreciate something that you have to wait for or have to struggle for.

Our courtship was a fine example of this. When I started teaching at Cradock High School in 1982, I was warned against a certain good-looking young man who was allegedly only after one thing when it came to girls. I was petrified of him and adamant to keep a good distance. However, being a small town, the young people all frequented the same social spots and inevitably that caused us to mingle often. Clinton, an eligible bachelor who was never short on ideas concerning the opposite sex, held an annual party at his apartment at the beginning of each year. He would then invite all the bachelors and new teachers or nurses. Everyone got to meet the new talent in town and he had a chance to grade them as well.

When he came to my apartment to invite me to his party, I politely, but firmly, declined the invitation. I was not going to be part of any local talent show. Long afterwards he told me that he thought I was very snobbish and that he thought to himself, "Girl, in this town you are going to meet your match!" He said that, at the time, he didn't know it would be him!

The other teachers at school assured me that I should come along to meet everybody. It was always a wonderful get-together where new friends were made. I decided to go for a little while only. At the party I met a very pleasant and attractive young man, Louis Copeman, who invited me to dinner over the weekend. We went to the Masonic Hotel where, of course, the whole gang was present. Sitting next to me at the ladies' bar counter, was yours truly. Something funny happened and Clinton started laughing. This was no ordinary laugh. He bellowed like a lunatic and promptly fell off his barstool and landed on his back on the carpet, still screaming with laughter. I was sure everything I had heard about this wild man, was true. Definitely not my cup of tea!

As I got to know him better, I realized he was actually one of the few guys who were pretty honest and not at all pretentious. I enjoyed his company, but was still not interested in going out with him. When he invited me to the rugby dance five months later, I didn't know how to decline without sounding too rude. I accepted and hoped that I would be able to find a good excuse in time. However, I accompanied him with trepidation, waiting for him to make one wrong move to justify asking him to terminate our date. He turned out to be the perfect gentleman and never tried to make a move on me. I was impressed.

After that evening, he came around regularly, but I wouldn't let him touch me. I still didn't trust his intentions. As time went by, I was shocked to find myself looking forward to his visits. I tried to fight off this feeling of attraction and convinced myself I really didn't like him. The more I pushed him away, the harder he came after me. His determination was a quality I admired. He remained the gentleman I had got to know and I couldn't deny the attraction any longer.

He took me to meet his mom and sister, Gigi, who was visiting with her new baby, Kate. After an evening with them, I realized he came from a top class family and could then understand where his impeccable manners were bred. After our engagement, I found out that his paternal grandmother, Gisèle, was the French Countess of Neuilly, now an exclusive suburb of Paris, who married a South African Captain, Vincent Rice, during the First World War. Her brother had died aged sixteen, so the title came to her, hence the double-barrel surname, de Neuilly-Rice, which was passed on to her two sons along with the title of Count. Clinton's maternal grandmother was Kathleen Werdmüller von Elg, whose father was a Swiss Baron. This wild man of mine had blue blood running thick through his veins.

Three months after our first date, he asked me to marry him. I accepted and we were married on 18 December 1982. The best mistake I ever made!

"Clinton and Cecile on their wedding day"

My host country, Botswana, taught me patience, perseverance and determination. I realized that I could do anything if I put my mind to it. I had crossed rivers that could not be crossed, drove in a two-wheel drive where only 4x4's could drive, created a luscious garden in the barren, dusty stretches of the bush with water we had to siphon out of a seemingly dry river bed. My children were happy and healthy despite the absence of medical care. We were such a happy, close family and blessed with so many friends and family who loved us.

One afternoon I was looking for Gisèle, who had been gone too long. Gobopamang told me that she had gone to the river with Diranga (Clinton). I walked down to the river and saw the little inflatable dingy far upstream. On closer inspection I saw Clinton and Gisèle floating down river in this little contraption. They were having fun trying to steer the boat to avoid floating debris. When they got out they were covered in mud, but had had the most enjoyable time. The special bond between father and daughter grew ever stronger.

Two weeks later we had another storm. Clinton was in town and found the river in flood on his return. One of the workers rushed up to me and dragged me to the river. All around I saw the others running to the river shouting the message that Diranga was going to swim across the raging current.

The noise from the rushing waters was too great for me to hear what Clinton was saying to our neighbour, John Smith, on the opposite bank. I shouted and gesticulated wildly in an attempt to convince him to stay over in town, but he could not hear. When he started stripping off his clothes I knew there was no stopping him. He pointed up stream towards the pump house and I realized what he was about to do. We stared in horror as he dived into the crazed waters in his boots and underpants. He started his epic swim upstream with the current sweeping him towards the confluence of the two rivers. Uprooted trees and branches were swept along at speed in the river and some narrowly missed Clinton's head as he was swimming across. I stood transfixed, horrified and speechless. I could not see any human being making it unscathed through those waves and the rocky outcrops. If the tree trunks splintered against the rocks, how could a human body survive?

I had a long rope on the back of the pick-up, which we threw at him. He grabbed hold of it and we started pulling him towards the bank. He was exhausted and needed to pull up his underpants, which were now down to his knees. He was trying to tell us to stop pulling, but we just wanted to yank him out as quickly as possible. The result was a naked Clinton standing on the bank of the river, panting for breath, too tired to care about his audience watching in their multitudes.

He seemed uninjured and my immense relief turned to anger as I considered the irresponsible act and its possible consequences. I got into the truck and drove the hundred meters home, leaving him right there. He slowly walked up the hill, straight into the shower and then collapsed on the bed. His heart rate was alarming, but he was even more upset that I had just driven off and left him to walk. I could not explain it myself, just that I was furious that he had played with his life. I could not bear the thought of losing him. Later that evening he felt better and said that he would swim across any river to get to me. I couldn't help falling in love all over again with this daring, courageous man of mine who so readily expressed his love for me.

The staff thought Clinton was a super human. Stories about his swimming across a mad river in flood soon spread throughout the region. Of course everyone added spectacularly to it and later even we laughed at the wonderful tales. Some folk believed he might have walked across on the water. Petty theft on the farm stopped for a while!

The hot and humid conditions after the rains were very conducive to the breeding habits of the putsi flies. It was an impossible task to keep the children from taking off their clothes. Gisèle was told to keep her panties on, but Michael was only happy when he crawled around stark naked. Putsi flies are large flesh coloured flies continually in search of warm damp places to lay their eggs. As stated earlier, all washing had to be ironed to kill eggs that might be present on wet clothing hanging on the line.

I noticed a small black spot on Gisèle's upper arm, which she kept on scratching. It was a putsi that had hatched under her skin. Gobopamang showed me how to squeeze the worm out. It was still alive and wriggling and I felt revulsion at the sight of the worm. We killed it and disinfected the tiny hole in her skin. She must have picked it up in the damp sand pit where she always played.

Into Africa

The poor dogs also had many putsi lumps under their skins and had to be sprayed to keep them from further infestations.

The iron we used for the laundry was filled with hot coals, so our clothes always smelled of smoke. When the river came down in flood, all the water we pumped into the tank was muddy and our clothes became discoloured.

After six months in Botswana, during the flooding season, I was offered a lift to Johannesburg by our dear neighbours, the Smiths, who regularly flew to South Africa to collect spares for their quarry machinery. They owned Nata Quarries which supplied sand and crush to the copper smelter in town

Dick and Florence Smith, a middle-aged Scottish couple, lived about six kilometers downstream in a large colonial style house on the bank of the Motloutse River. This couple was so good to us and Gisèle soon spoke of Oupa Dick and Granny Smith. We were having sundowners with them one evening when this unexpected invitation caught me off guard.

I said the kids and I would love to fly down with him the following week. We would then fly SAA to Cape Town to see my parents.

"Lassie, I am flying first light tomorrow morning and then we're off to Zambia for a long time. Make sure you're there if you want a lift to Lanseria."

Impossible, I thought. Our washing still had to be done and I needed more time to prepare for the journey. It was to be tomorrow or much later.

When we got home I had to make the decision quickly. I didn't want to leave Clinton without having stocked up the pantry and without proper instructions to the staff on how to care for the garden. I was excited about seeing my parents again, but hated leaving Clinton. He made it easier when he said I should go and

45

take a well-deserved break. He would be fine and promised to check on the garden. Time would fly and we'd be together soon again.

I hauled out a suitcase and started packing the couple of clean items and a full suitcase of washing! What on earth would my mother think! The next morning early we were ready to board the twin engine Baron at Selebi-Phikwe airport. I had so much to tell my family in South Africa and Gisèle was very excited to see Oupa and Ouma again. Still, I couldn't bear the parting and tearfully said good-bye to Clinton. Three weeks would speed by.

CHAPTER 7
A FLYING JACANA

As we circled above Selebi-Phikwe en route to Johannesburg, I was surprised to find how I attached I had become to life in the bush. I looked down at the ugly town and marveled at my ability to adapt and survive.

We landed at Lanseria at 08h00. From there I got a taxi to the Rotunda. My two bush babies and I boarded a bus to Jan Smuts Airport (now Oliver Tambo International Airport). I have to remind you at this point that we stood out like sore thumbs. Our clothes smelled of smoke and our dress code was distinctly out-dated. Michael cried for a feed and I slipped him under my top as casually as I could. Nobody noticed until his suckling noises became very pronounced. I pretended I didn't care and to be honest, I didn't really. Two ladies on the bus looked disapproving and shocked. The rebel in me stared back at them and they continued their gossip privately. My baby was hungry, had never taken a drink from any other container except what nature supplied me with, and what else was I supposed to do? I missed the bush already.

A kindly old gentleman took pity on us and offered Gisèle an ice cream. Being male he obviously didn't see the folly of his generosity. A toddler of two and a half and a dripping ice cream in a bus spelled disaster. By the time we arrived at the airport, all three of us were smeared with chocolate and ice cream. What a mess, I thought, and was grateful that I knew nobody. All I longed for now, was my beautiful Cape Town, a hot tub and my mother's tender, loving care.

I had no pre-booked tickets and worried that the flight to Cape Town was sold out. I carried Michael, held Gisèle's hand and paid a porter to carry my suitcase. Gisèle needed the toilet just as the long wait in the queue was nearing its end. I had to take her, trust that my luggage would not disappear and join the back of the queue again. In the ladies room I glanced at myself in the mirror for the first time in months. I had become lean and tanned, but my clothes were baggy and I did not resemble my usually groomed self. I would think of something before I saw my family, I thought.

The ground hostess informed me I was too late for the 13h00 flight to Cape Town and would have to go on stand-by for the 15h00 flight. I went to the phone booth to phone Alta, my sister in Cape Town. I only had Botswana currency with me, and one 50c coin that would buy me approximately a minute's airtime.

When she answered I had just enough time to say, "Please fetch me at DF Malan Airport at 17h00 this afternoon. No, I haven't left my husband and nobody is ill. Just be there." We were cut off and I could imagine her confusion and concern.

The next challenge was the two-hour wait before our flight. Gisèle ran off every now and again to explore this noisy, unfamiliar terrain. I would follow, carrying my baby and the huge nappy bag. Michael's diaper had to be changed and I had no disposables with me. In those days disposable diapers were expensive and only for high days and holidays. By the time we boarded the plane, I was utterly exhausted. I longed for Gobopamang to hold Michael and for Clinton to hold me.

We boarded and I sat down with a sigh of relief. At least I could not lose Gisèle in the building now, and the flight would only be two hours. Michael sat on my lap, dribbled, baby talked and removed the last traces of my lipstick with his grubby little fingers. He had left fingerprints all over my top and reached out to touch everything else around him. After take-off the hostess served tea. This was tricky with a groping baby on my lap, but I was determined to enjoy this welcome treat. Gisèle ordered tea as well, much to the amusement of the hostess. Gisèle had an amazing vocabulary and soon had the dear lady under her spell. She had spilled half her cup over herself and surrounded herself with cookie crumbs. Thinking I needed a break, she took Gisèle to show her the cockpit.

The crew was most amused when she said the plane was just like the African Jacana (a lily trotter bird on the swamps). The male Jacana raises the young and carries them under his wings with only a bush of dangling legs visible, while foraging for insects on the floating leaves. She had seen this on a visit to the Okavango Swamps and thought the aeroplane carried its passengers in much the same way. The co-pilot thought her delightful and rewarded her with a chocolate. When Gisèle was brought back to me the hostess related their interesting conversation in the cockpit. Gisèle was thoroughly enjoying all the attention and I was happy until I saw the chocolate in her hand. Were these people not trained in child behaviour? Chocolates should only be given to kids outside where they could mess to their hearts' content. But, what the heck, I looked like a hooligan already. She asked me if we lived in the country. My first reaction was defensive. I didn't always look like this.

We landed in Cape Town and the familiar smell of the sea breeze awakened my homing instincts. The strong South Easterly wind blew away all my fatigue. I have always loved Cape Town and its soil felt wholesome under my feet.

We waited till last to disembark. By this time I just wanted out. I had another nasty stare on the descent when I nursed Michael to ease the pressure in his ears. Just before I became angry, I realized that six months ago I would also have stared with disapproval at a breast-feeding mother in public. I did cover him with a baby blanket while nursing him, so nobody could see anything. It was simply the idea that shocked people. In the bush everybody breast-fed their babies. There you were regarded with disdain if you did not breast-feed. It was the most natural thing in the world, not something that you should be ashamed of! How far had our norms migrated from the good and wholesome!

I gathered my children and started towards the reception area. The expression on Alta's face spoke volumes. She only recognized us by Gisèle's gait. She looked worried and without much ado rushed us to her car. Once at her townhouse, she ran a full bubble bath, ordered us all to get in, and proceeded with operation clean up. Once the children had been fed and put to bed we relaxed with an ice-cold glass of Rhine Riesling. I had to get dressed, do my hair and make-up and look presentable. Whatever for? I objected. We were ready to go to bed! But, I must admit, it did feel good to be groomed again.

She wanted to know everything. Once I started, I sounded like a machine gun rattling off. I was careful to focus on the fun and not on the hardship. She worried enough about us. We laughed and joked until late. The dust, spiders, snakes and slimy bovine hides seemed light years away.

The wind in Botswana is conspicuous in its absence. In Cape Town it is a constant. Instead of being annoyed, I welcomed the afternoon winds in the Cape. It blew away the pioneering cobwebs in my mind and seemed to cleanse my soul of the dust of hardship.

The following day Alta's poor washing machine was assaulted by our discoloured clothing. Alta was a teacher at Lilliput Pre-Primary School and I spent the morning trying to soak away the ingrained muddy residue in our clothing. At the same time the children wanted to be outside. I ran around like a headless chicken. I really appreciated my staff in the bush for the first time. I missed Michael's "Gogo" and Anna's help. The next day Alta took Gisèle to school with her and I could cope better. When she came home at midday, we left for Bredasdorp.

My parents were thrilled to see us. Gisèle ran straight to the sweetie cupboard and Michael was only happy in my arms. These people were strangers to him and there were no black people around. It was also too cold for his liking. He took a while to settle down.

I had to tell them all about my life in Botswana. Where I tried to spare them, Gisèle embroidered, and eventually they knew out of the mouth of babes came the truth. She sat on her grandfather's lap and told him about the geckos in her room, about the cobra I had shot in the garden and the night watchman who always slept on duty. She had given them a detailed account on what had happened in the Post Office, the way mom moaned and swore when she picked up skins at the abattoir, and about our crossing the river in the tractor. My mother was horrified, but my dad laughed and said he could relate to many incidents seeing he started off his farming career in Rhodesia as a young man. He told us about the way he had made bricks to build his first home and about the many absurd situations he had had to face as a pioneer. I could hear that he still cherished his memories of those old days.

I always got on very well with my father. We understood each other and he believed in me. He was always ready to encourage me and I knew his advice was sound. He used to say that "common sense ain't so common" and that a clever person could learn from his own mistakes, but a genius would learn from other's mistakes. He was a good judge of character, but not too critical or judgmental.

I do recall, however, him saying to me one day after a conversation with an acquaintance, "If I could buy that guy for my price and sell him for his price, I would make a fortune."

Many of his sayings still make me smile today. He only wore natural fabrics and disliked synthetics intensely – he called them plastics! He never drank from a mug and insisted on a cup and saucer. He also believed that true insight was rooted in simplicity. Any fool could complicate things, but it took a genius to simplify. Here he would always quote Einstein's theory of relativity. He believed if you could not express an idea, you didn't understand it. Another one of his favourite quotes came from Proverbs 16:18, " Pride goes before destruction, a haughty spirit before a fall."

I recall the day Clinton asked him for permission to marry me. Having made a name for himself as a keen starter where women were concerned, Clinton had my mom worried. My dad, however, liked this gutsy young man and told my mom that you could tame a tiger, but it was impossible to put a backbone into a jellyfish. She was still wary, but I think she understood better when she recalled her memories of my dad as a young man.

Clinton used to tell our friends that my mom told him that he was a womanizer and that a leopard does not change its spots. She made sure he knew she'd be watching him! My mom turned out to be the one who spoiled him rotten.

I spent the most wonderful three weeks with my parents. I was faced with another good-bye and quietly contemplated on how many times we put ourselves through this painful ritual. Does it ever become easier? I couldn't wait to see Clinton again, but I knew the bush, with all its surprises, was waiting to test my courage once again.

CHAPTER 8
COMING HOME FROM HOME

My heart skipped a beat when I saw Clinton. I had missed my soul mate tremendously. We had become one in every sense of the word. It was wonderful to be pampered during our holiday in civilization, but I couldn't live without Clinton. I realized that I was so blessed to have this man at my side. He loved people and socializing, cared deeply for his family and made me feel so special.

Apart from his excellent physique and good looks, he was one of the most sincere and loyal people I ever knew. He would walk that extra mile for a friend, even if it cost him dearly. He had a wonderful sense of humour and was so easy to please. He didn't ask a lot from life and was prepared to give all. He was also very direct. I often asked him to refrain from using that f word, but he could say it in such a way that it sounded merely descriptive and not offensive.

Another attribute was the fact that he was not easily offended. I think he was so comfortable in his own skin that he couldn't really care what others thought of him. He never tried to impress people, but he had huge influence on people. You had to be very rude to him before he felt offended.

He had the most amazing ability to speak to people on their level. When he spoke to the farm workers he knew they understood that if something was broken, it was fucked. When he spoke to Janis Sylas, he sounded just like a Greek. When he spoke to his mother, he used the Queen's English.

Clinton grew up in the Karoo with English as his mother tongue. At primary school all his friends were Afrikaans and he became completely bilingual. He was teased at school for being a Rooinek (English speaking South African) and his mom had to sew on buttons to his school shirt every day as he fought for his heritage. When he went to Grey High School in Port Elizabeth, he was called a Dutchman because of his Afrikaans. He was pretty confused about the whole language thing. In those days there was still a great barrier between Afrikaans and English folk in South Africa, possible because of the Boer War a century ago.

The boys also fought about the make of car your dad drove and what political party he belonged to. Clinton used to say he had no chance of avoiding a fight as his dad drove a Fiat, was English-speaking and voted SAP (the South African Party started by Jan Smuts). Most people in Cradock drove Chevrolets or Fords and voted for the Nationalist Party. The boys had no idea what the difference was and obviously only echoed noises they heard at home. FC Grobbelaar, Clinton's friend, used to stand up for him. FC's dad also voted SAP so they joined forces in one out of three fights. These two were born an hour apart, FC just before midnight and Clinton just after. They remained close friends throughout.

In his first letter home from boarding school he complained that this Rooinektaal (English) was very difficult. However, he established himself as a very well balanced young sportsman and pupil and went on to become head of his house in his final year.

He always spoke fondly of his old school and made sure Michael was booked to go there nine years ahead of time.

Clinton was quick to apologize when he believed he was wrong. This quality endeared him to everyone. I remember being angry with him about something and all he did was look at me.

"Why are you staring at me?" I demanded.

"Can't a cat look at a queen?" he asked and smiled.

How could I stay angry with him? As soon as he saw me soften, he would ease up to me slowly and kiss me. All would be forgiven, far too easily!

If this sketch makes him look too innocent, I apologize. He was naughty, fun-loving, impossible, stubborn, loving and kind and very inquisitive. Our children adore him and happily obeyed him.

Because of his nature, we made many friends everywhere. Our friends came over regularly for a barbeque and a chuckle. Some Sundays Leslie Hutchinson, an English lady from town who had a secretarial services business, and who insisted on wearing her fancy high heel leather shoes, would hop across the river from stone to stone, clutching her bottle under her arm, to visit us. She had the gift of gab and we could sit back, relax and be entertained by all her stories. On her return journey she would inevitable slip on the rocks and fall in the water. We would know this by her use of the f word ringing out loudly in the riverbed.

" Oh f…k, me leather shoes!!"

Gisèle could never understand that Leslie only fell on her way back.

Mary Hehir, a South African lady who married an Irishman, lived in Selebi-Phikwe where her husband and his partner ran a very successful construction company. Everybody spoke about this wonderful woman and I could not wait to meet her. One evening a couple arrived to visit. I was introduced to Mike and Mary Hehir. We got on like a house on fire. She became a very close friend and a regular visitor to our farm. Michael called her aunty "Mely".

Her grandfather was the famous Jan Smuts, international statesman and prime minister of the Union of South Africa. I thought of the photograph in my parents' home where my dad, at the age of six, stood next to this famous general in front of the town hall in Colesberg. My father had the greatest respect for this far-sighted statesman who was years ahead in his thinking.

Mike, a tall man with a strong Irish accent, had the most infectious sense of humour. He could tell the funniest Irish jokes at his own expense and he could keep amazing rhythm with a couple of spoons in one hand. My children were captivated by this spoon act and often tried to imitate Mike, but without any success.

A week later Mary brought along two friends, Ann O'Connell and Leslie Frost, for afternoon tea on the farm. I suspect a sense of curiosity played a part in that first visit. I really liked these girls and welcomed female company.

My lawn had come along very nicely, despite the fact that our mode of mowing was a small mesh enclosure with three sheep. As they grazed one section short, we moved the pen for them to "mow" the adjacent part. Their mowing was irregular and depended on their appetites. Mary thought this hilarious and presented me with her old Briggs & Stratton 2-stroke petrol lawn mower. This was an enormous gift and changed the face of my garden.

Picnics on this freshly-mowed carpet became a favourite pass time and the children played on the lawn with Clinton showing them how to do cart wheels and arab springs. He was so athletic that I regretted never having had the opportunity to see him in action as a gymnast and rugby player. I met him when he was twenty-nine.

He had broken his leg in a motorcycle accident and never did sport competitively after that.

I was so chuffed with this lawn mower and did all the mowing myself. Clinton smiled and tried not to burp at the same time. Bliss was watching him cavort with the children on the lawn. Michael screamed with delight as he was thrown high up in the air. Gisèle tried everything her daddy did and showed no fear as he swung her around. "Another wild one?" I wondered.

The lack of finances in our lives did nothing to dampen our spirits. We had a healthy, happy family and really enjoyed spending time together. Our commitment to each other was the basis from which we drew strength and hope for the future. Because of the unpredictable nature of our situation, we had little routine and enjoyed each good moment fully. Michael grew up feeding whenever he was hungry. Till the age of two he used to run around and play and take a short cut to find me whenever he was thirsty. My dad used to tease him about it, but he just covered his eyes with his little hand and helped himself.

My children ran wild, climbed trees and had the river and the bush as their playground. They learned about traditional life in Botswana at the cattle posts. They ate maize porridge with sheba (tomatoes, onions and cabbage lightly stir-fried) with their Motswana friends.

One of our neighbours was an old Mosadi (lady) who tilled her land with a hand-held plough pulled by an ox. After the rains Clinton went over with our big tractor one evening and ploughed the land for her. What would have taken her a week, he did in two hours. Michael sat on the back beneath the bright lights shining all around the tractor and watched the old lady scattering her maize seed on the freshly turned soil. There were mosquitoes and other flying insects milling around his head, but he just loved being on the tractor. His birthday cakes for the next couple of years all had to be tractors, first a green tractor, then a red one, then another colour. One day he went to sleep in the canopy of the tractor because he was afraid he'd miss out on the next trip. He would sit in the tractor all day with Tapologo Koontse when there was plowing to be done.

George McAllister hunted for hares at night with his hawk-eagle. One evening we accompanied him on a hunt. His hawk-eagle would sit on his arm and dive-bomb down on a hare when the spotlight found its prey. George would then allow the bird to kill and eat a little. The dead hare would then be loaded on the pick-up and the search for another would begin. The tiny bells fastened to the feet of the eagle would enable George to find it easily in the dark. Hawk-eagles don't usually hunt at night, so this was a unique experience we all found quite fascinating.

My dad encouraged me to video this as he said it was simply unheard of. It was amazing to see the crop expand to about four times its original size as the bird devoured its prey. Gisèle always felt so sorry for the hare. George and Fred Harrison sometimes stopped by to take us on an eagle hunt, much to Gisèle's distress and Michael's liking. Boys and girls are simply different in their make-up. The male is born a hunter and the female a protector.

Both Gisèle and Michael grew up close to nature and appreciate all the links in the eco chain. Even ants had their job cut out for them when ostrich eggs had to be cleaned out. Clinton would drill a small hole in each egg, shake out the insides and leave it next to the ants' nest for these industrious little creatures to clean it out, which they did in three days.

My children never felt deprived in the bush. They were free to roam around, play in the sand, swim in the river (when it contained water) and ride their bicycles. They were exhausted after a day's play and slept through at night. They were generally very healthy and didn't know what a doctor was, until Michael developed a very high fever one day.

I took him to Dr Frank Fox, a doctor at the BCL (mine) hospital, who diagnosed tonsillitis. However, he thought his temperature was far too high and decided to check for meningitis, seeing that there were numerous cases around. A lumber puncture was the only way to draw fluid from the spinal cord. I was horrified at the thought and called on Mary for moral support. She joined me at the hospital and reassured me of Frank's credentials. I remembered Hettie's warning to check that all needles used were opened in front of me. It was traumatic for me to hold down my baby for Dr Fox to insert the needle between the vertebrae. Michael was screaming and I was crying my heart out. What a sight we must have been. I stayed with Michael in the hospital overnight and the next day the tests came back. He did not have meningitis. I was both relieved and furious that my baby had to go through all that pain for nothing. At that moment I was ready to attack any doctor who came near me. I just wanted the uncomplicated, wholesome bush where the only pain was the absence of comfort.

The staff, who adored Michael, gave him a hero's welcome. I was deeply touched by their concern and appreciated these kindly souls anew. I did not have electricity or any modern cons, but I was surrounded by people who cared for me and that meant everything. I thought of how I used to take everything for granted, how self-centered I was, how utterly unaware I was of the things in life that really mattered. May be the bush saved me from myself.

Whatever the reason, my pride was being subdued by humility. This was good, necessary, painful and embarrassing.

CHAPTER 9
OPERATION THIRD WORLD

Our original plan in Selebi-Phikwe had been to raise ostrich breeding pairs and export them to America. We had orders for seven pairs at $70000 a pair. Because of the interference by the South African Ostrich fraternity, we were unable to get export permits from the Department of Wild Life, even though they still maintained we would be allowed to export live birds. Someone in the Department had obviously been persuaded to stall the process.

In the interim we planted cabbage and other vegetables to sell locally. The seedlings had to be imported from a reputable nursery in South Africa. The applications submitted for import permits were often misplaced and communications in Botswana were slow and tiresome. Everything took a long time – Africa time. The locals often reminded us that we were without patience. We would not live long if we stressed so much. Why rush something that could be done the following day? Why did the white man always want everything quickly? Life was a long walk and rushing was not good. We needed a paradigm shift in our thought patterns.

The Botswana Government regarded some immigrants with suspicion. Many came to make a quick buck illegally without ever putting back a thebe in the hand that fed them. One could understand why they were cautious, but that didn't help our cause. We were producing food for the community and thought we should be helped, not hampered.

No official was prepared to take a decision without the consent of his superior – and there were many superiors, so the buck was passed. These delays caused such inefficiency that we were often exasperated. But, when in Rome do as the Romans do.

We realized our ostrich export permits were going to be stalled for a long time. Clinton could put his pilot's license to good use to earn an additional income. He started flying PriceWaterhouse accountants and other executives all over Botswana. This stint brought along its own adventures I shall recall at a later stage.

We received regular visits from the elderly Chief of Mmadinare district, who was also an uncle of Seke's. Chief Kidwilliam had a young wife who came from Bloemfontein in South Africa and small children. His weekly visits were informative and encouraging. He was of the old school and a traditionalist. Their young son carried the royal birthmark above his left ear and his proud father never failed to point this out. He was a descendant of Sir Seretse Khama and thus of royal blood. My children loved him and would sit on his lap and listen to the many wonderful stories he told them. They enjoyed playing African hopscotch with his children and were always so pleased to see his truck driving up to the house. They would pepper him with questions about the bush and he would patiently give them detailed answers.

After one of his visits, I was deep in thought about what was happening to us. Here was this dear old man whom we adored. He felt like a grandfather to me. A mere two years before I would not have believed that I could feel like this about a black man.

He was sincere, gentle and wise. I had grown up to believe black people were too different from white people to converse with one another so freely and honestly. I was being liberated of my preconceived ideas that colour separated people. He would socialize with us, but not necessarily with our staff. The class barrier was far stronger than the colour barrier.

I wondered about South Africa. There were many changes taking place and many previous laws segregating people were being revised. How long will it take to break down the suspicion that existed among the different ethnic groups? As long as there was a lack of understanding of and a lack of respect for one another's cultures, the antagonism would continue. People within the same ethnic group could differ completely. That is what makes humanity so interesting. We tend to generalize so easily and believe that all Xhosas are like this and all Zulus are like that and all Tswanas are something else, instead of looking at individual characters. There are so many misconceptions between races, languages and cultures that nations have missed many opportunities to build together, and have concentrated on their differences rather than their similarities.

In South Africa, for many decades, English and Afrikaans speaking people did not really mix. The same hurts and joys are experienced by people across the board. The problem lies with our ignorance of one another's ways.

Leah, a large woman who came to work for us, had her two children living with her. They came with her every day and also became my children's friends. One day, as the happy little group came back from the river to have their supper, I was just about to take my children for their bath. I noticed they were already dressed in their pajamas and spotlessly clean. Leah had taken all the children to the river to bath them there. They smelled of Lifebuoy soap and decided they would take their baths in the river every evening instead of in our reed bathroom. I sent their shampoo and lux soap with them after that and thanked Leah for her efforts.

One day I went to watch this ritual and discovered there were many other mothers close by also washing their children in the river. Happy sounds of children laughing echoed across the twilight sky. The picture of happiness so touched my heart that I could not help smiling and feeling the most wonderful sense of peace in my heart. It took so little to make these people happy that I felt ashamed of the many demands I made on life. It is so easy to be happy, but we often think we need so many other things to accomplish this level of content. The more we have, the more we think we need.

Our presence on the farm sparked the interest of John Motang, head of the CID in the area. He frequently popped in to check on us. His first visit came shortly after the Bezetto's were spotted on our farm. This couple farmed in the Mmadinare district. Their movements were monitored by the local CID for reasons not known to us. We believed Mr. Motang's interests were to protect the community and we answered his questions without reserve. He probably investigated our motives for farming here as well, seeing that there were many con men operating under the cover of small businesses. Be it as it may, we experienced his concern positively and he knew he was welcome to see us whenever he so wished. He also occasionally warned us when there were undesired elements in the vicinity. He did not like the idea of me staying alone on the farm when Clinton was away flying. I decided to stay with Daan and Julia Pelser in town from then on, whenever Clinton was away from home.

CHAPTER 10
BOOMBOO'S FIRST VISIT

In preparation for Clinton's mom's visit, we were scurrying around fixing little things that needed attention. The door of her bedroom, for example, was the lid of a wooden crate in which a stuffed lion was transported. This door hung on homemade hinges and closed with difficulty. The gap between the floor and the door was large enough for any nocturnal visitor to crawl underneath, so we simply dropped the door to leave the gap at the top instead. Lyn was at peace with all of God's creatures and had no fear of spiders and the likes, but we thought it would at least look better.

Boomboo is Lyn's nickname and all her grandchildren and children call her by this name.

The lawn was mowed and the veggie garden weeded. The staff was looking forward to meeting her and did their best to help tidy up the yard. Clinton fetched her in Johannesburg with the plane and she landed in Selebi-Phikwe in style, only to be surprised that her transport to the farm was in the tractor. She burst out laughing and saw the reason when they had to cross the flooding river.

Her reception on the farm was royal. The staff stood lined up to greet the Mosadi Mogolo (elderly lady) from Cape Town. She was, after all, their grandmother too. She was quite taken by all the attention and I was hoping that her first impression was favourable. After a drink under the shade of old faithful, she could contain her curiosity no longer. She wanted to be shown around immediately. Clinton obliged and the rest of us trotted along too. She was impressed with all our hard work, but added her suggestions on how to improve things quickly. She simply loved the reed bathroom and paid it a visit. Tapologo had started the pump in the river to fill the tank overhead and had forgotten to switch it off. The tank overflowed and my mother-in-law was literally caught with her pants down while the overflow drenched her. The only way to tell when the tank was full was to wait for it to overflow!

Being the sport she is, not even this mishap could spoil her mood. We entertained her on roast fillet and vegetables and she was most impressed at the cuisine from our primitive kitchen.

The following day she presented me with fruit and vegetable seed she had brought from Zimbabwe where she had just spent her annual holiday with her mom and sister. Joan Howard, Lyn's sister was headmistress of Chisipite Junior School in Harare and Kathleen Sykes, Lyn's mom, lived in Marondera, 60 km outside Harare. Her older sister Lee Duncan, was the MP for that area and a thorn in the flesh of corrupt officials in the government of Zimbabwe. She was forced to leave Zimbabwe a couple of years ago and emigrated to Ireland where she lives today. There were rumours of her life being in danger and she decided to leave the country she had served so passionately for many decades.

They were all keen gardeners and I was so excited to get this seed in the ground. Boomboo was going to make sure we would have enough vegetables to survive. Soon she had planted the seed in neat little seedbeds under the shade cloth. Before the end of her visit she had the pleasure of seeing most of the seed germinated and peeping through the top layer of soil.

Gisèle appeared at the garden gate with a dead cobra dangling like a necklace around her. Boomboo was horrified and only calmed down when she saw the snake was dead. I didn't know what to say. She had other toys to play with, but was obviously more interested in the things nature provided to create a stir. Michael was in his walking ring, charging along the narrow footpath in front of the house until one wheel hit a bump and the whole contraption fell over. He landed on his head and sported a lump and blue mark for a week. I decided it was much safer to let him crawl and pick up the occasional thorn.

One evening while I was bathing Michael in the tub in my bedroom, I heard this almighty thump and the whole house shook. I shouted for Gobopamang to see what had happened. She ran to me and reported Gisèle's first car crash. The pick-up was parked about a meter from the wall and she had turned the ignition switch on. Because of the automatic choke, and the fact that it was in gear, the vehicle lurched forward and hit the wall. She was fine, apart from a bump on the forehead. The pick-up, though, was not going to heal by itself. The damage was more cosmetic than mechanical, but we realized the folly of leaving the key in the ignition. We would have to think more pro-actively now that she was growing up. I wondered what else lay in store for us in the next twenty years.

We flew down to the Tuli Block to see other ostrich breeders. The closest registered landing strip was near Mahalapye on a private freehold farm. After a couple of hours we returned to the plane to find the tyres deflated. Clinton saw that the tube valves had been removed. He was furious. Our host took us to the owner of the farm who expressed complete surprise at this nasty act. It turned out that his wife had removed the valves to discourage any future use of their airstrip without explicit permission from her. They were wealthy farmers and this malevolence was uncalled for. The valves were returned without an apology and we took off feeling

Into Africa

disgusted. The last of the daylight was fading fast and our safety on landing had been compromised by an unnecessary and unkind act. I started trusting and liking black people more and white people less – a gross generalization at the time, but that was just what I felt then.

We were sad to say good-bye to Boomboo the following Monday, but she had inspired us by her positive example and I marveled at how blessed I am to have such a wonderful lady as my mother-in-law. No wonder my husband was such an extraordinary man of courage and kindness.

"Gisèle in the Lethlekane River"

CHAPTER 11
MURDER ON THE RIVER

It was with shock and disbelief we received the tragic news of the death of Chief Kidwilliam. How could anyone want to hurt this gentle soul? He could not have had enemies, or so everyone thought.

The mere idea of murder in this peaceful area was disconcerting to us. Everybody's nerves seem to be shot as interrogations by the tribal police and the soldiers became more intense. The Officer Commanding came to see us to give us this sad news.

While crossing the river one evening, the chief and his two small children had an "accident". He was missing and the two children were asked to tell their story. The police realized that something was wrong, as there were many conflicting stories from the villagers.

The BDF (Botswana Defense Force) and the police started a search all along the banks of the Motloutse River in an attempt to recover the body. After two days Lynn Smith noticed an unfamiliar sight on the opposite bank of the river. She informed the police, who confirmed the bloated body belonged to the chief. The body was taken to Mmadinare where the unofficial interrogations left a couple of people near dead, but revealed the true circumstances of his death. The traditional system was fast and effective. The murder of a member of the royal family was extremely serious and was dealt with in a different manner.

In Botswana the dead are revered and treated in the most respectful way. Support for the bereaved family is astonishing. Family members would gather at the deceased's home with food and take over all household duties. The children are taken care of by aunts and grandmothers, and the men would sit around and recall the greatness of the person who had passed away. The gathering would traditionally last for at least two weeks. Here, sorrow is comforted by helpful actions, not flowers or cards. Compassion for the bereaved is real and dealt with in a real way.

Gisèle and Michael were mercifully too young to conceive the horror behind it all. They were just puzzled that their friends and their father did not visit us again.

Clinton attended the funeral, a gathering of royals and loyals. He had also attended another royal funeral a while before, where many cattle were slaughtered and food provided for the people in attendance. This funeral of an uncle of Seke's, was held in Serowe and Clinton flew down in the Baron. He had to wear a suit and tie and we searched the still unpacked boxes to find suitable attire. His belt was missing and there was no time for further delays. Clinton rushed off with a string of orange baling twine holding up his suit trousers. Seke insisted on him joining the royal family and VIP's on the specially erected podium at the gravesite. He declined politely, but Seke sat him down next to him. It was terribly hot and most of the men took off their jackets. Clinton refused and suffered the heat stoically.

Seke indicated quietly to Clinton that it was quite acceptable to take off his jacket. Clinton opened his jacket slightly to show Seke why he could not possibly remove his jacket, and Seke had to exercise all control not to pack up laughing. This piece of rope had cost him much sweat and had provided the substance for a new story that had the Khama family amused for a long time.

On landing at Selebi-Phikwe, he took some of the ground crew at the airport for a flip. Most of them had never flown and this little jaunt elevated them above the rest. You had either done it or not. Nobody spoke about the terrified shrieks up in the air as Clinton did a couple of sharp turns and dives. Since then he was treated with special consideration and affection by his "ground crew" where clearing immigrations became a painless exercise from that day on.

CHAPTER 12
A CLOSE ENCOUNTER OF THE AFRICAN KIND

Sekghoma Khama and his Zimbabwian girl friend, Catherine, were visiting us on the farm. During supper that evening we heard a strange cat-like spitting from under the shelf rack. Lisa, our Staffy, was barking and going mad. I thought one of the kittens was the object of his aggression and stooped down to save the poor thing. As I reached under the shelf to grab the cat, Lisa went berserk and Catherine shouted a warning. I jumped back just as the shield-nose struck out at me. These snakes are pretty venomous. I vaulted over the low wall behind me and stood there in complete shock. My first thoughts were of my children. Because it was cornered and felt threatened, the snake prepared to strike again. I had to get the dog away from the snake. I was petrified it would disappear into the house where my children were sleeping. On a burst of adrenaline I flew to the bedroom, grabbed the shotgun and passed it to Clinton through the window.

It was too dark to see properly as the snake withdrew into a dark corner, but Clinton took a shot and hit it. It came sliding out and a second shot finished it off. I felt nauseous. At once I became furious at life. I longed for civilization and wondered how long we would have to put up with this kind of primitive lifestyle. My old fear and hatred of crawlies surfaced violently. Why can't we just live somewhere safe like normal people! This adventure had gone too far and I was ready to voice my previously suppressed fears and worries. When my family was endangered I resembled a lioness with cubs, ready to lash out and fight. So much for thinking I had settled down in the bush!

Clinton saw how upset I was and held me tight. He could offer no guarantees that this sort of thing won't happen again, but he would be there to protect us! I calmed down in his embrace. He knew me so well and didn't offer any promises that he wasn't sure he could keep, but his mere calmness brought hope and peace. We loved each other and needed each other. This had to be enough for now. The rest we would work out as we went along.

For a while I pitied myself, wondering what other woman would have been prepared to put up with such incredible everyday inconveniences. Had we lived in a tropical rain forest that was at least beautiful and bountiful, I could imagine surviving, but this part of Botswana was ugly, dry and as hot as hell. Trying to make a living here was hard enough without having to fight off venomous monstrosities as well. My anger was spent and I composed myself sufficiently to face our guests again.

The next day I greeted an old lady on her way to the river to fetch water for her household. She carried a large bucket on her head and smiled cheerfully despite the many kilometers she had walked. I felt ashamed of myself yet again. Complaining was so easy and gratitude so difficult when your frame of reference was so different. I knew then that happiness was a choice independent of circumstances. I could choose to focus on the positives and live a life of hope, or focus on the negatives and become a pain in the backside to all around me.

I wondered what the locals really thought of us. Did they see our endless rushing as madness and a disturbance of the peace, or did they envy our ability to make things happen fast? They could endure the heat and accept the wild animals more readily, but is that because they didn't know a different way of life? The more questions I asked myself, the less I understood.

My impatience at the slow pace of my gardener got me going. I wanted to plant more grass and needed the surface prepared. The only tool I had was a pick and shovel. I took the heavy tool and started picking the soil like a possessed person. I would show my staff I was prepared to do what I had asked them to do, and in half the time too!

After two and a half hours of lifting the pick and swinging it down into the soil with exaggerated energy, I had completed the tilling process and started leveling the ground to plant the runners. I overheard the other workers in the maize land expressing their admiration and surprise at the strength of this white woman. I had proved that I could work hard physically and at the same time I had exhausted my frustrations effectively.

That evening my hands were blistered, bleeding and swollen, my back hurt and every muscle in my body ached, but I fell into deep sleep of content. Clinton merely shook his head and wondered why I hadn't just given the job to one of the men. There I was, tired and unwilling. I should use my head more than my hands, he said. Gobopamang told Clinton that he must not make Mma Rice angry, because she saw what I could do with a pick!

After that day Ipotseng never complained and did her gardening work diligently and faster. Even the workers on the land speeded up when they saw me approach.

A week later my hands were healed and we received guests from Taiwan. They were Mr. Robert Lee's representatives and we planned a weekend safari to the Tuli Lodge in the Mashatu game

Reserve. They had never seen elephants or other big game and were very excited on their first trip to Africa.

Billy Gold, owner of Texas Air, offered us his twelve-seater plane to fly everyone down to the Tuli Block. His wife, Pat, and their three children accompanied us on a most enjoyable and exciting weekend.

The flight took twenty minutes as opposed to a two-hour drive. Two armed game rangers met us at the landing strip and we were taken on our first early morning game drive. Cobwebs were still glistening from the dew and we saw a couple of insects flying into the webs. They were swiftly attacked by the huge spiders. I tried not to look too closely.

At the Tuli Lodge we were received in style. This beautiful lodge is an oasis of green lawns and indigenous trees and shrubs in the surrounding dry bush. The gong summonsed us to a hearty breakfast in the lapa.

After breakfast we went on a long game drive. The children were excited about the laden picnic hamper, which included fizzy drinks they were not usually allowed.

On rounding a bend we heard the sound of branches breaking. We stopped and watched an enormous elephant bending down branches to reach the sweet new growth on the tips. The beautiful tree was soon destroyed and broken branches, stripped of its leaves, lay scattered all around. The ease with which this giant snapped thick branches was awesome. The Taiwanese visitors could not believe the strength of the African elephant.

We saw many kind of buck grazing lazily in the veld. Occasionally one would leap off into the distance, displaying its grace and agility. We returned to the lodge exhilarated.

Later that afternoon Clinton accompanied our visitors on another game drive. They were armed with video cameras and zoom lenses to capture some of these magnificent animals on film. They were in their element, but out of their environment, as was soon evident.

When they had not returned by eight o'clock that evening, the home ranger became worried and radioed them. There had been an attack by an elephant and the guide had lost his way. They eventually found their way back via other bush roads.

Our guests were so pleased and excited about their adventure and Clinton needed a drink, fast. There and then he decided that was his last game drive with these gentlemen who had no idea how close to death they were.

The story of their trip was both hilarious and frightening. Because of a previous encounter with elephants in Zimbabwe, Clinton had lots of respect for them and preferred a good distance between him and these huge beasts. The Taiwanese were the opposite. They could not get close enough. When the elephant resented their close proximity, it started to charge. The driver then stalled the engine and Clinton, who was sitting at the back and therefore closest to the charging elephant, clambered hastily towards one of the front seats. He was met, mid-air, by Mr. Ching and Mr. Ling who were rushing for the back seat to get better footage of the elephant. Just before the elephant could join them on the back seat, the Land Rover jerked back to life and they sped off into the bush with the two Asian gentlemen still hanging over the back seat taking video shots.

Clinton asked them later if they had taken a good shot of the elephant's tonsils!

CHAPTER 13
A LONG AWAITED INSPECTION

We continued working hard and hoping harder. We refused to give up on our dream to export ostriches.

One of our female ostriches got hurt. Her neck was cut on the wire fence. Clinton saw Dr Keith Scott in town and asked him to come out to the farm to have a look at the wound. It may seem strange that our GP was asked to help with an animal's injury, but there was no veterinary surgeon in Selebi-Phikwe. Keith was an excellent doctor and kind enough to oblige. Keith and Linda Scott brought their three children, Robyn, Damien and Lulu with. Linda home-schooled her children and believed in a very hands-on approach. These children were bright and stimulated and therefore interested in this little outing.

When Clinton took them to the ostrich camp the female was standing there grazing happily on the lucerne land. This hardly seemed like an emergency to Keith, until he saw the food simply falling to the ground from the gaping wound in its neck. The neck was perfectly stitched up and the ostrich could carry on with its life.

Into Africa

The next bit of exciting news was that my mom and sister were on their way to visit us. I was thrilled and at the same time I realized that our dwelling might be a culture shock to them. I looked at our khaya and was grateful for my garden, which served as a reasonable camouflage for the dismal little pondok. We hastily whitewashed the walls and varnished the reeds around the bathroom. I even put an arrangement of flowers in their room and the bathroom. Desperate times called for desperate measures. I pulled out all the stops.

On their arrival I watched closely for any indication of approval. I did not want them to feel sorry for me. I wanted them to believe as desperately as I did that things were going to be all right. I needed that emotional support so badly.

Alta's giggles told her story. My mother looked around, cleared her throat and said, "Mmm…..very interesting."

I took that as a positive sign. They admired the garden, but eyed their bedroom door with suspicion. Crawlies had free access here and they shared my fear of spiders. The mosquito nets over the beds brought a little comfort, as I could tuck them in at night in an impenetrable cocoon. More giggles came from the bathroom.

My mother has always been a workaholic of the worst degree. I think housework was therapeutic to her. When my dad had a house built for them in Bredasdorp, he had it fitted out with pure new wool carpets as he knew only top quality flooring would be able to survive the onslaught of her favourite appliance–the vacuum cleaner. Here in the bush we had no electricity and I knew she would be frustrated with our methods of cleaning and maintaining acceptable levels of hygiene. She was going to have to relax and simply enjoy the change of scene, I was hoping.

The tranquility of the bush and the absence of electrical cleaning appliances soon managed to do the impossible. She started to relax and enjoyed the children playing around her. I took her tea under the tree and enjoyed this new mood of contentment I saw in her. She was having a good rest here and I was thankful for that.

We had been invited to dinner at the Bosele Hotel by some overseas business people. The group consisted of people from different ethnic groups, different tongues and different countries. The elderly, distinguished looking white German gentleman was married to a black Zambian lady, another white guy had a wife of mixed origin and the young man at the head of the table was a Communist from Yugoslavia. All these factors were unacceptable to the South African conscience at that time. I anticipated moral disapproval from my mom and Alta. However, as the evening progressed, everybody relaxed more and we all had a good time. The next day, of course, we had a long discussion about the dinner. We laughed about the way my mom had experienced this mixed group. She still could not understand or condone this sort of thing. She did admit that the conversation was very interesting and educational, though.

I took them to meet Mary, Hettie and Gerhard and Julia and Daan. They liked my friends and felt I had a good moral support system in place.

Their visit ended all too soon. I knew that the happy time we spent together would soften my mom's report to my dad concerning our standard of living. Alta must have felt very wealthy when she returned to her beautiful townhouse in Cape Town.

CHAPTER 14

KALAHARI CASCANADES

Financially the battle became intense. Seke had decided it was taking too long to make money with ostriches. He wanted a rental per month for his ground instead of a share in the business. We could hardly make ends meet as it were, so it was impossible for us to pay rental as well.

Eventually, after many visits to the capital Gaborone, Clinton managed to get a permit to export 30 chicks to a monastery in Cyprus. The Abbot wanted us to send 4 chicks initially to see if they could be raised successfully. The chicks were crated and flown over after we managed to collect a full file of permits and certificates. The trial was successful and the Abbot gave the order for the rest. We were told the permit was for a single shipment only and were not allowed to send the balance of the order.

We just knew that there was outside interference involved. Two South Africans came to see us and offered us two prime farms in exchange for all our ostriches or a written commitment that would prohibit us from farming with ostriches in Botswana. We refused, out of principle, to be bribed like this. The Botswana Game Industries were offering us a third of the market value for our skins. They sold only to the South Africans who in turn controlled the world market. It was so frustrating and we knew we had a fight on our hands.

Clinton decided to form an association through which to work. All game farmers were invited to join to give us more clout with the Department of Wildlife. As a united front we stood a better chance.

Clinton was given a permit to capture wild ostriches in the Kalahari Desert and started rigging himself for this operation. We had two guys working for us who came from Bokspits in the southern Kalahari area. They knew ostriches and were not afraid of them. They also knew the desert well and proved to be invaluable during the capture. Willem Esterhuizen also had a drivers' license and could drive the big truck back from the Kalahari.

I had to organize the food supplies for the week-long expedition in the desert. I had decided not to join them, as sleeping under the Land Rover did not especially appeal to me. My life was primitive enough where I lived.

Clinton chose to sleep under the vehicle as he could stretch out more comfortably than inside the Land Rover. At the same time he was able to defend himself against the inquisitive hyenas, which preferred to hunt at night, true to their sly natures. He could hold on to the chassis when he felt one pulling at his boot and kick it away with the other foot. They were so tired after a day's capture that they would eat and pass out at night. Goodness knows what other dangers lurked while they were asleep. When I heard about the hyena incident from Freddie, Willem's brother, I was really happy I had stayed home with my children. Freddie said Clinton's boot had connected the hyena on its nose before sending it off into the night. The hideous laughter of the scavenger rang out across the desert plains forlornly.

Dirk Botha, a friend of ours from Bloemfontein, accompanied Clinton on the following trip. His two young sons Adriaan and Floris, aged nine and seven, went along too. I did offer to keep the children with me, but they were more interested in spending time with their father who was always very busy back home.

As they filled up with fuel at the Selebi-Phikwe Filling station before the trip, Daan asked them where they were headed. There was no way he was going to miss this outing and loaded his food (a bag of potatoes, a crate of tomatoes, a bag of onions, ten kg maize meal, oil and plenty of meat) and his sidekick and off he went with them.

Daan was famous for his snoring and Adriaan and Floris gave us hilarious descriptions of their evenings in the truck with Daan. Apparently Dirk, who had chosen to sleep under the truck too, jumped up and knocked his head against the under carriage. He urgently asked Clinton if he could also hear a lion roaring. Clinton pointed up and told him not to worry, it was only Daan's normal nocturnal sounds. Daan could shame a lion.

Daan was allowed to go with on condition that he sat in the back. The tinned food cans went flying around him as they sped along the tracks and he wasn't too impressed. I think this was the first time Daan was happy to come home after an adventure.

Clinton, Dirk and the children were filthy when they arrived back on the farm. None of them had had a bath for a week. Their clothes were stiff from the dust and grime, but they had also enjoyed the experience tremendously.

A while later Anthony Norden from Manchester, England, was sent to Selebi-Phikwe to keep an eye on a clothing factory in which his mother had invested a great deal of money. It was his first trip to Africa. He landed at Selebi-Phikwe airport with Air Botswana and from there he flew with Clinton and a party of businessmen to Shakawe in an eight seater plane. Tony had never flown in a smaller aircraft than a Boeing, so Air Botswana already had him a little nervous. He was very apprehensive when he boarded the Cessna.

The flight over the Kalahari Desert was daunting; the landing even more so. Tony was appalled when he thought Clinton was going to land the aircraft on the road, but completely lost it when he saw Clinton was going to miss the road. He jumped up and tried to grab the joystick to pull up the plane. His fellow passengers grabbed hold of him and forced him back in his seat. He went berserk when the plane landed smoothly next to the road —on the real landing strip that happened to be slightly camouflaged by the long grass around it. He felt ill and thought these Africans were mad.

Once out of the plane, he couldn't believe his eyes when he saw a vehicle approaching. Their hostess had arrived with sandwiches and tea. This all in the middle of nowhere! Nothing made sense any longer.

Later that afternoon they were taken on a booze-cruise on the Okavango River. Everybody was relaxing and enjoying another exquisite African sunset. After dark and en route to the camp, Tony asked about the shiny objects in the water. He was informed they were the eyes of crocodiles and hippos. He laughed at this ridiculous story and implored their hostess to tell him the truth. She steered the river barge closer to the bank where she shone the spotlight straight on to some crocodiles. A fascinated Tony immediately took some photographs. He just knew nobody in Manchester was going to believe this. The boat was now directly opposite their camping site. Vere van Heerden, a helicopter pilot, decided to be helpful and lifted a meter long croc out of the water. He held it by its tail and head for Tony to get a good close-up shot. When Tony turned around he was shocked to find himself sharing space with a real live crocodile right in front of him. He was not going to stay on the same boat as a crocodile and jumped ship without hesitating. He ran, swam and thrashed through the water towards the bank. According to the men on the boat he just about walked on the water in his desperate flight to safety. He might even have stepped on a couple of surprised crocodile heads! He never even noticed the scores of crocs around him in the water. He headed straight for the bar and ordered a triple. His first day in Africa had him suffering from severe culture shock.

He had just downed his drink and was telling the amused barman about the crazy people on the boat. He turned around and saw the same crocodile come swaying into the bar! He landed on the bar counter screaming. Vere had carried the young crocodile up from the river and released it at the bar entrance. Clinton and the other guys followed Vere into the bar and were laughing themselves silly. The croc was returned to the river and everybody settled down with a cold beer and some more hearty laughter.

At this stage nature was calling and Tony excused himself to have a leak outside. The next moment he was back, white as a sheet and stuttering. He saw a tree and did a wee against it. The next moment the tree walked off and he realized he had had a leak against the leg of a hippopotamus. Everyone packed up laughing. He was either drunk or still in shock. Even the old bush hands thought this preposterous, until they went outside to check out his story. Sure as anything, there they saw the heavy imprint of a hippo foot and right next to it a wet patch. Everybody agreed that Tony had had a most exciting introduction to Africa.

On his return to England nobody believed him and he was nicknamed Crocodile Dundee by his family and friends.

After a couple of months he returned to Botswana with his wife, Deborah. The first facts she wanted to establish were the details of Tony's first day in Africa. Clinton retold the story exactly as it had happened and Tony beamed from ear to ear! At last his amazing tale was verified and his wife was impressed, to say the least.

CHAPTER 15
A MIRACLE AND KUBU

It was time for my annual visit to Bredasdorp. I had managed to buy two tickets on the night flight to Cape Town. Even though I was excited about my visit, it was yet again hard to be separated from Clinton for three weeks. We were such a close unit that it was painful to operate separately.

Michael was now two, but I had not weaned him yet. On the plane he asked for a sip. I covered him with a baby blanket and he was just about to start feeding when he peeped out and looked down the aisle.

"Won't the people laugh at me?" he asked.

"It doesn't matter one little bit, my boy," I assured him.

Some of my friends used to tease him about the fact that he was still drinking from me. He has a mouth full of teeth, Julia said. Won't he bite you? I knew Michael would never hurt me if that meant a rationing of his favourite food.

I was no good at this weaning stuff. I simply could not see the point of it. It was good for my baby and for me. I knew that he would be weaned before he went to school. The bond created between mother and child during breast-feeding was so special that I did not want to stop for the sake of stopping. My mother helped me to wean Gisèle and she would have to help with Michael too. He was a sturdy little boy even though he did not eat enough solid food while feeding from me.

"Hey Musimane! What are you doing!" my dad used to tease him. "Taking a bit of a chance, are you?" he playfully asked me.

I was not feeling all that great when I arrived. A slight nausea, totally out of character for me, made me go for a check-up. Dr Christa Retief, a lady doctor in Bredasdorp, asked me some questions and decided to do a pregnancy test. I laughed at the suggestion. It was impossible for me to be pregnant. Michael was taking too much from me and, besides, I had an intra-uterine device, which was supposed to be totally effective. I was absolutely stunned when the test was positive. She proceeded with a routine examination. When she pressed down on my abdomen, I felt a sharp pain. This worried her and she wanted to a scan to detect a possible ectopic pregnancy. I was sent to Cape Town. The scan showed a dark spot near the left ovary and there was no clear sign of an embryo in the uterus. I was rushed off to the Vincent Palotti hospital in Pinelands. The surgeon explained that he would perform a laparoscopy, remove the IUD and, if necessary do a D&C. I trusted his judgment and agreed to the operation.

Gisèle, Michael and my mom stayed with Alta. The weaning process was forced on me unexpectedly. Michael was upset. I was tearful and felt helpless. My mom and sister were wonderful. That evening she rocked Michael to sleep and comforted him when he cried for me. We had never been separated before. My world was in turmoil and all I wanted was my husband and his comforting arms to hold me and tell me we'd get through this one as well.

I woke up to find the doctor at my bedside. He explained that he had removed a small growth on the fallopian tube, but had decided to continue with the D&C. He felt that it would be the best under the circumstances. He was sorry I had lost the baby. Clinton was two thousand kilometers away and I was still reeling from all the happenings of the past couple of days.

Lyn and Gigi came to see me in hospital. They were so supportive and I appreciated my family all the more.

After this ordeal I went back to Bredasdorp and was recovering quickly. Alta and I took my children and my brother's three children to the beach at Arniston. It was a lovely autumn day and the kids really enjoyed playing in the sand. Michael wouldn't leave my side and still tried to convince me to allow him a drink. It was his first visit to the coast and he eyed the waves suspiciously. He would venture closer to the water and run back when he saw a wave breaking and washing out to shore. Gisèle, true to her nature, was not daunted by anything and followed André into the shallow water.

Michael ran to me and exclaimed in his African accent, "The reever, it is coming closer and closer!"

Alta and I burst out laughing. I hugged him and tried to explain the ways of the sea. He didn't trust this crazy motion one little bit and would not go near the water. Eventually I carried him to the water and gently lowered his feet to feel the cool water and foam swirling around his legs. He still did not trust the scene and quickly curled his little legs up and around me like an octopus. He was a real bush baby and happy on solid ground in excruciating heat among his little black friends.

Back in Botswana I still felt a little nauseous and thought my body had not come to terms with the fact that I was no longer pregnant. My hormone levels were obviously still unbalanced. I continued with my everyday chores of gardening, doing the books and running my household. After another six weeks I felt a lump in my tummy. I knew it was just the scar tissue from the four-centimeter cut that had thickened.

Another month later, while I was in town and visiting Mary, Ann happened to be there too. She was a qualified hospital sister and I told her about this lump. She made me lie down on the bed and pressed down lightly on my tummy. Her eyes widened she and told me to go to Dr Scott immediately. I was a little surprised, as I was feeling good, but Mary phoned Keith and he said I could come to the surgery right away.

Keith Scott, who had been informed of the whole episode in Cape Town, examined me and declared in his usual relaxed voice that I was nearly five months pregnant. I nearly fainted. He got on the phone to Basil in Cape Town.

"Basil, I have one of your patients here with me."

"How is Cecile?"

"Very pregnant, but in good health," Keith said.

There was this long silence before the good doctor exclaimed, "Impossible. Absolutely impossible!"

Well, I sat there wondering what incredible things were happening to me. This baby had survived a scraping of the uterus by an experienced doctor held in very high esteem throughout the medical world. As stunned as I was at the news, I was also extremely worried about the health of this new life I was carrying. There had been so many interferences, both surgically and medicinally during the first crucial trimester.

Keith calmed me down and told me that our bodies were made to cope with a lot more than we gave it credit for. If this baby had survived so far, it was surely a little fighter and would be fine. I am sure he was also concerned, though, but his calmness helped me incredibly. Basil wanted to see me immediately, but we told him 2500 km were just too far. I would see him when I went to Cape Town for the birth. He promised to take care of everything for me.

I rushed off to Hettie's shop where I knew Clinton was sending a fax. He looked at me with that typical smile of his. When I told him the story, I saw him speechless for the first time in many years.

He looked at Hettie and said, "Only a prize bull could manage that! Seems to me I only have to walk upwind from you and pollination takes place."

We became excited about the new baby and started thinking of names. If it were a girl, we could call her Charlotte, I said.

"Absolutely not! Before I met you I knew a loose girl called Charlotte."

"What about Maud?"

"That sounds too sad."

So I continued until I realized Clinton had know far too many "easy" girls in his hay day. We still had enough time to think of a name. Clinton thought it might be a boy, in which case we would name him after a grandfather.

Even better, we could name him Clinton, I thought, seeing that he was such a little survivor!

Two and a half months later, at the end of September, was President's Day long-weekend. Clinton suggested we take a gentle trip up to Nata, overnight in one of the chalets at Nata Safari Lodge and take a look at the thousands of pink flamingoes on the pans close to Nata. I was more than seven months pregnant and fairly uncomfortable already. However, we needed a break and I thought this would do us the world of good. Nettie McLean, an

Into Africa

American friend of ours, was involved with the Peace Corps and carried an Embassy Card as a member of the diplomatic corps in Botswana. She wanted to go with us. At the many roadblocks en route, her status and card proved to be a great blessing, as we were waved through by the BDF soldiers and escaped the long queues of cars awaiting inspection of license discs etc.

After admiring the awesome sight of thousands of beautiful pink flamingoes around the saltpan, we arrived at Nata and had a drink in the open-air ladies bar. Of course we had to run into some friends who were on their way to spend the weekend on Kubu Island. George and Pat McAllister asked us to join them. Clinton thought of my condition and declined out of consideration for me. When we were told it was an easy two-hour drive away, Clinton looked hopefully at me. I had never been to this island with its famous petrified Baobab trees. I had only seen it on a television advertisement by the South African transport giant Spoornet.

Kubu Island, as described by Michael Main in his book "Kalahari", is known to only a couple of hundred people. " It is situated in the South West of Sowa Pan. Kubu is an outcrop of ancient rocks, a small island, rising no more than 20m above the plain, beset with grotesque, stunted Baobabs. Gnarled, usually leafless, their dwarfed and twisted forms suggest the agony of ages spent on salted waters beneath a remorseless sun.

A careful search of the shore will reveal minutely chipped Stone Age tools. The utter desolation and almost pre-historic atmosphere on Kubu touches your very soul."

Here in the bush we measure distance euphemistically in terms of hours to keep the morale high. We had enough food and fuel for two days, so we considered the option. The only worry was my delicate state.

Nettie was sitting in front with Clinton in the Land Rover 110 station wagon and Michael and I sat on a soft sponge mattress at the back. Gisèle had been invited to spend the weekend with Daan and Julia in Pretoria where they were planning a fishing trip next to the Apies River. Michael enjoyed having us to himself for a change. I felt reasonably comfortable at the back, but wasn't sure about spending two more hours in the heat and on the road.

The decision was taken. We would go. We drove northwards on the road to Maun for a while and then took a dirt road left that would take us to Kubu Island. The name sounded romantic and I envisaged cool waters lapping the ancient shores of this tiny island.

The dirt road became a track, which became a succession of corrugations in the ash-like soil. The vehicle was vibrating seriously and Clinton slowed down. The powdery ash, kicked up by the moving vehicle, slowly started overtaking us and filtering into the cab. We couldn't close the windows because we did not have air conditioning and the heat was intense. As we continued I saw Clinton and Nettie turning gray. The soda ash in the air made it difficult to breathe and I held a handkerchief over my mouth. I tried in vain to get Michael to do the same.

I felt the first contractions play over my stomach. When I mentioned this, Nettie swung around in a panic and asked for a double gin and tonic from the cool box. She had never delivered a baby and was not going to attempt this cold stone sober. We stopped and after Clinton and Nettie had finished their gin and tonics and Michael and I our cold drinks, we continued. We were sure we were more than half way to Kubu, so it would be better to continue rather than turn back. The road was so terrible that we wondered if we had lost our way. In the distance Clinton spotted a hut and there we enquired where we were. The old man walked over slowly and could barely understand us.

"Auk, Sa. Now you are here."

Into Africa

This answer would normally have brought the house down, but we were tired and fed-up and realized we were not going to find answers. When Clinton asked where Kubu Island was, the old man merely shook his head. This told me we still had a far way to go. I was exhausted, but there was no way I was going to have my baby in the middle of the Sowa Salt Pans! We pushed on and tried to be as positive as we could.

Eventually, after four hours and a couple of dust devils, we arrived at Kubu Island. "Island" being the inoperative word. There was no water in sight, only the forlorn red Baobabs that resented our presence and ignored our disappointment.

We parked next to one of these petrified Baobabs to set up camp for the night. There was no sign of any other living thing – no flies, no mosquitoes, nothing except absolute silence and desolation. What the hell, I thought. All this way for this! No wonder nobody ever came here.

Michael looked up at me and asked, "Mommy, why do you look so strange?"

One look at him and I understood his concern. His eyes were the only part of him that was not gray. His entire body was covered in ash. I turned to Clinton and Nettie. They obviously came from the same planet as this little alien. I looked at myself in the side mirror of the Land Rover. I could be that cute little alien's mother.

I started laughing. The more I looked, the more I laughed. I laughed until I could no more. I sat down on a stone and held my tummy as I laughed. Clinton and Nettie looked concerned. Nettie said that this behaviour could be the prelude to labour. That stopped my mirth in its tracks.

I was adamant that I was all right. I just needed Clinton to pour some water over me so I could clean off the ash and I would be as good as new. Clinton announced, regretfully, that we could not use our water supply to wash. We needed it for the next few days to survive. We were in the middle of the dry saltpans and anything could happen – a puncture or something similar. I took a cup of water and tried to clean my face.

We collected some wood for a fire. Nettie erected her one-man tent and Clinton decided to sleep on the mattress next to the vehicle. I was preparing my bed in the Land Rover where Michael would sleep with me under the net in case the insects only came out at night. All I needed was rest. I wasn't hungry at all. I fed Michael his favourite cereal and milk and put him to bed. Clinton and Nettie were still enjoying their drinks and avocado ritz, which Nettie had prepared. Imagine having this tropical delicacy in the middle of the most desolate and dry place on earth! Imagine ice-cold gin and tonics with sliced lemons!! We were all too tired to cook anything else and the fire died a slow death. A liquid diet was far more to their liking at that stage. The two of them started talking about their school days and the one story became more incredible than the next. I was sure the heat, ash and liquor had caused their brains to function below par.

Eventually Clinton asked me to go and lie next to him on his mattress. I wasn't too keen, as I didn't know what lurked around in the dark night. After several pleas I obliged. We were admiring the stars and unwinding after the long day. The next moment I felt something running lightly across my chest and swollen stomach. I screamed and jumped up. The big, hairy hunting spider had already disappeared in the dark. I thought if this baby were not born right there and then, it would most certainly become the toughest child in the world.

Inside the vehicle I tried to sleep, but my mind refused to switch off. The hyenas could be heard for miles around. They were laughing at these crazy humans intruding on their territory. There was no surface water for hundreds of miles on these stretched out barren plains of saltpans. Everything was void of any type of life-giving

Into Africa

fluid. The red Baobabs were stretching up their branches in a silent prayer for rain. This was a God-forsaken place.

Some evidence could be found to support the theory that there were people living on Kubu in the year 500 AD. Apart from this historical significance, I failed to understand the attraction Kubu Island held for many.

I woke up a couple of times to check if Clinton was all right. Hyenas would often bite their victims in the face and Clinton was well enough anaesthetized to sleep through it all.

I was grateful enough when first light appeared. We had coffee and drove off in the general direction of the Boteti River, hoping to find it without getting lost again. Clinton's sense of direction was very good and we set out on a positive note. Simply leaving Kubu was a good enough reason for me to optimistic. I think I might have experienced this place quite differently, had I not been pregnant, uncomfortable and covered in ash.

After a couple of hours we came to a halt in front of a game fence. What now? We had been traveling southwards around the fringes of the Makgadikgadi pans and we knew our direction was correct. Without a word Clinton and Nettie got out and simply cut through the fence for us to go through. Once on the other side, they took great care to mend the fence again.

After another couple of hours we hit the tarred road that took us from Mopipi to Rakops and the Boteti River.

When we stopped under the enormous old Scotia tree on the bank of the Boteti River, we all shouted for joy. I grabbed some shampoo and Michael and I ran into the river to take a bath. The cool water washed away all the ash, sweat and exhaustion of the last few days. We splashed and played like happy children on a picnic. All clean and refreshed, we settled down to some cold drinks under the tree. The setting sun had transformed the thorny landscape into a beautiful orange watercolour. We decided to overnight right there. Clinton started a fire to prepare for our barbeque.

All of a sudden we heard a stampede coming our way. We had chosen a watering hole as our campsite. All the local cattle and goats came charging down the embankment and headed for the water right next to us. The goats in front were shoved deeper into the river by the cattle at the back and some were forced to swim around or drown. In their quest for water, some of the animals had trampled others mercilessly. When they had had their fill, they slowly turned and headed back to their kraals. A couple of cattle still milled around and eventually plodded up hill and away.

Within a space of twenty minutes the pristine picture had been turned into another cloud of dust and dung. Nettie and I agreed that we had seen enough of the bush to last us a lifetime. We were ready to head home.

Nettie slept in the Land Rover that evening and Michael and I slept in the one-man tent. Clinton pulled up his mattress next to the tent and dropped off to sleep immediately. I felt quite safe in the little tent once I had zipped it closed. The mattress on which Michael and I slept was a two inch thick inflatable with a leaking valve. I woke up occasionally with a very sore hip. I would then blow out my lungs to inflate the thing again, only to wake up to a similar situation. I gave up and fell into an exhausted sleep.

I was awakened by a strange chomping sound close by. I tried to wake up Clinton. After several tries he woke up. He sat up, listened and said it was only a hippo grazing in the shallow waters. This enormous beast was feeding only fifteen meters away and I was expected to go back to sleep! I didn't want to think what we would look like if this hippo trampled on our tent. My young son and unborn baby! Nothing would be left of us. Clinton replied that the hippo was unfamiliar with nylon and would see our tent as a solid structure to be avoided. If anything, I should be more

Into Africa

worried about him sleeping outside! I resigned myself to our fate and listened to Clinton's snoring on the one side and the hippo's chewing on the other. I tried to shine the torch through the net window in the tent to monitor the hippo's movements. The battery eventually gave up the ghost and I mercifully passed out too.

The next morning we were like homing pigeons, desperate for our own place and took off eastwards. That afternoon we dropped off Nettie at her home in Selebi-Phikwe. On our arrival home my khaya seemed so luxurious. I stood under the shower for ages and became really grateful for small mercies. This was the closest I came to loving this pondok.

When I fetched Gisèle from Daan and Julia the next day, I told her what a lucky escape she had had. She grinned and exclaimed that her weekend was great! The most exciting part of her weekend was when Oom Daan bumped the gas bottle into the deep side of the Apies River. He needed it to cook his catch. His son-in-law Kobus was forced to don his wet suit, aqualungs and flippers to retrieve the bottle. All was forgiven when the smell of fresh frying fish filled the air. She was so amused by it all, especially the way Oom Daan had bullied Kobus into make the dive.

Two days later Nettie arrived on the farm with a new Peace Corps worker from America. We were sitting at the table where I was peeling fruit. She told us that the entire Boteti River region was infected with the bubonic plague. The river was home to hundreds of crocodiles, especially there where we camped. Apparently the crocs waited for the animals to come to the water to drink. Many goats and cattle had been taken prey by the crocodiles there. I reflected on our frolicking in the Boteti at sundown. We were in the perfect spot at the right time to supply these ugly reptiles with an easy meal. That area was also inundated with malaria carrying mosquitoes.

I looked at Clinton accusingly and executed a mock attack on him with the knife in my hand. He pretended fright and leaned back sharply, snapping the leg of the chair. He went down like a bag of potatoes on the kitchen floor. Before he could get up, the Peace Corps worker had fled the scene. Nettie tried to explain that we were only joking, but she had seen enough and refused to unlock the door of their vehicle. Nettie had to take her back to town immediately. I think she left for America shortly afterwards.

Clinton and I thought it very funny. We laughed about this incident for a very long time afterwards. Our sense of humour was a clear sign of how far we had gone off the track of normality. It sure helped to be a little crazy in the bush.

"May be I should have given you a little nick on your arm to teach you a lesson," I said.

"Then I would have punished you with the family weapon again," he laughed. Where on earth did I find this man!

CHAPTER 16
DELIVERANCE

It was November and the heat was unbearable. I was getting ready to leave for Cape Town to have our baby sometime in December. I had no idea of my expected date of delivery. Imagine that! The scan would have to give us an estimate.

The baby was very active at night and kicked so hard that Clinton often woke up when I lay behind him with my tummy touching his back. I had also had the odd contraction. I think the intense heat had something to do with that.

We decided that I should fly down ahead of time to prevent any further surprises.

My brother had been praying for us faithfully. He knew we were struggling financially and was also concerned about our spiritual well being. He had posted me a whole box full of faith books to read. I knew about his faith in the Lord. I also knew that he was being ridiculed and persecuted by many of his friends and family for daring to speak out so boldly for Jesus. Many people thought he had been dragged into some kind of cult.

I was a little skeptical when I picked up the first book. I didn't want to become a Jesus freak. I still believed that a person's faith was a very private matter between you and God. I felt that it was more important to lead a good life than to try and convert people to Christianity. Everybody had their own way and had to be given their own space to work out something for themselves. I had been confirmed and accepted as a Christian at the age of seventeen by our Church. Surely I would go to heaven because the church had given me a certificate confirming my faith. I led a good life and tried to teach my children good values.

However, I found these books so easy to read and so encouraging that I could not stop. I was reading the sinners' prayer printed on the last page one evening after everyone had gone to bed. I did not really consider myself a sinner. Sinners are people who do bad things and don't believe in God, I thought. But something inside me prompted me to read it out aloud. As I finished this prayer, something happened to me. The most wonderful sense of peace flooded my heart. I could not explain it. I just knew God was right there beside me. I could reach out and touch Him, I felt. I had never felt this way before, nor experienced such closeness to Him.

I started reading my Bible and discovered many truths about salvation. I also discovered that much of my thinking had been warped by dogmatic church teachings. I shuddered when I read that good people don't go to heaven. Born again people do.

I had always disliked this term. It reminded me of those pushy Christians who rudely intruded my personal space in their efforts to "convert" me. How dare people assume that I was not saved or not a Christian? I had gone to church often and I believed.

"The devils also believe, and they shudder" I read in the Bible. What, I thought! Does this mean that you could still go to hell even if you believed?

I realized what had happened to me that evening I read the sinners prayer. That was the first time I had honestly and personally confessed my faith in Christ and His redemptive work on the cross with my lips and believed it in my heart. I had become born again by the Spirit of the Living God. I was shocked that it took so little from my side, because the Lord had already done everything on the cross of Calvary for my salvation. I was taught that you had to earn your way as well. The old saying, that you had to live a life of honesty and good works to be acceptable in God's sight, is the reason so many good people never become born again. Their self-righteousness deceives them into thinking that they are saved. This was so true of me.

I knew now that even my best work was not good enough to save me. I was indeed a filthy sinner before I had asked to be cleansed by the Blood of Christ and given my life to Him.

I wanted to tell everyone I loved about this new love and peace that gave me hope for the future. I wanted them all to be saved and blessed. It was impossible to love the Lord privately. This thing needed sharing. Not sharing would be the same as not caring.

Only your true friends will dare to tell you something they believe you should know even if that means risking your anger or your rejection of their friendship. This is the hardest part of being a loyal and honest friend. Confronting your loved ones with the truth is often hurtful. We don't enjoy hurting or upsetting the people we love.

Clinton noticed this new bounce in my step and a serenity that shone from me. In many ways he was an example to me of a man of faith. His positive energy and calmness sustained me throughout our trials here in Botswana. His child-like faith in the ability of God always amazed me. I shared my life-changing experience with him. He listened intently. He could sense the peace and joy

I felt and was happy for me. He was, however, skeptical about this born again thing.

I felt a need to go to church and I spoke to Mavis Sweet about the Phikwe Family Church. I was not very keen on the happy clappy church, but she encouraged me to come along the following Sunday. I thought I would just check it out first.

That Sunday I sat next to Mavis in church. I was not used to people praising so freely. I had grown up in a church where everything was done in a specific order and where you were quiet and submissive. These people really enjoyed the praise and worship. There was no prescribed way and everyone moved their arms or bodies as they pleased. They were free to express their own personal love for the Lord by raising their hands or gently swaying to the rhythm of the guitar. I loved the atmosphere there and could feel the love of God all around me, even if this way was unfamiliar to me. I simply could not stop the tears. There you go, I thought. This is just an emotional sweep up. When I listened to Rod Talbot, the pastor, preaching from the Bible, I still cried. What now woman! Pull yourself together. Nobody minded my tears and I could not understand why I was crying. All I knew was that I felt the presence of God all around me. The message was about the everlasting love of God and how He never gives up on us even if we reject Him. His love is the one constant that cannot and will never change. He has chosen us, but it still remains our choice to accept Him.

I wanted to stay with Clinton as long as possible before flying to Cape Town, but he said that I should be near good medical facilities as soon as possible.

Keith gave me a letter to allow me on a flight. Usually you are not allowed on a flight if you are too far pregnant. We thought the baby was due late December.

Four days before I was due to leave I started feeling very ill. I experienced contractions and Clinton ordered me to bed. That evening it was so bad that I was sure I would give birth to my baby in the mine hospital in Selebi-Phikwe. We were worried. Because Michael was delivered by a Caesarian procedure, the doctors insisted I have another Caesar. Would this hospital be able to cope? Is our baby all right?

The following morning he took the children with him on his rounds to the ostriches so I could have time to rest. While lying down, I read about the healing power of God and that He healed everyone who ever came to Him for healing. There are 160 references to healing in the Bible. Matthew 9:22 read, "Take heart, daughter, your faith has healed you."

My faith in its fledgling stage was white hot and I lay my hand on my tummy and ordered my body to be perfectly healed in Jesus' name. I also asked the Lord to heal my baby in case anything was wrong with it. I felt better instantly. I was dumbfounded. Could this be true? You are imagining it. This is a perfect example of mind over matter. Some people could even bend a spoon from a distance by applying the power of their mind.

I got up and still felt good. Wow, I thought, a miracle has just happened! I went to the kitchen and started cooking breakfast for my family, the whole tutti–bacon, eggs, tomatoes and all their favourite stuff.

When they came back Clinton was very upset that I was not in bed. I told him that I had prayed for healing and that the Lord had been true to His word. I felt great. Clinton had been healed as a child after he was crushed between two heavy machines. He was in hospital for a long time and the doctors thought his paralysis was permanent, until his grandfather had come to pray for him. His recovery after that prayer of faith was remarkable. Not only could he walk again, he became a brilliant athlete, gymnast, swimmer and rugby player. He knew God could heal!

He put his arms around me and softly thanked God for this miracle. I wanted this moment to last forever. We stood together, enveloped in God's protection and love, so aware of our utter dependency on Him and so aware of our love for each other. It felt so good to be able to cast our cares on Him. Even if there were many more obstacles to overcome in the future, we knew we could do it all with God's help.

CHAPTER 17
THE COVENANT

We arrived in Cape Town and I went for a scan immediately. The baby seemed perfect and could be expected late in December. Dr Bloch was happy with my state of health and scheduled another consultation in two week's time.

In Bredasdorp relations between Andries and Christie were strained. They had had a stormy marriage and things weren't looking good. His faith had carried him through many difficult times, but also caused problems for him. Christie could not relate to his new commitment and enthusiasm for Jesus. She felt he had gone overboard and was too intense about his faith. We were all trying our best to ease the waters and protect their children from more stress.

I had listened to many people, preachers and churches. They all had their opinions and ever-conflicting doctrines. I had had enough. I wanted to read for myself what the Bible said about all of this.

I had to decide whether I would accept the Bible as the Word of God, and the only source of wisdom, so that I could make it my frame of reference. I asked God to teach me and lead me in truth. Once I started reading the Bible under the guidance of the Lord,

I could understand it for the first time in my life. It spoke to me clearly in every situation.

I stopped looking at Christians and started looking at Christ. I believed that every word in the Bible was true and powerful. My covenant with God was strong and unshakeable.

On Friday 1 December 1989 I paid Dr Retief another visit. She was the only local doctor who would perform an epidural anaesthetic and I thought it wise to have her as my stand-by. She was quite happy to help in case of an emergency.

On Saturday evening I started showing signs of labour. I did not want another Caesarian and thought I would keep quiet and see if I could deliver this baby normally. Gisèle's normal delivery had been so easy and I was sure I could do this again, despite the doctor's insistence on a Caesar for this one.

At six o' clock on Sunday morning my contractions were regular and strong. I went for a shower and got dressed. My mom saw me in the passage and knew something was happening. I told her to relax. I was only having a baby-something millions of women did every second all over the world. She wanted us to pack and rush off to Cape Town, a two-hour drive away. I told her it was too late. I had already disinfected the bath, put a sterilized pair of scissors and two pieces of string, to tie off the umbilical cord, in the bathroom. I was going to have my baby right there and then we could call the doctor. At least I would be spared the pain of a Caesarian operation.

She gaped at me with shock. Had I lost my mind in the bush? She started panicking and I sat her down next to me on the bed to pray God's peace over her. She never heard a word and kept up her appeal for me to go to hospital. Another hour later my contractions became very painful and my bravado lessened. All right, I would phone Christa.

Into Africa

Dr Retief told me to meet her at the surgery. I drove down in my dad's little pick-up. She had one look at me and told me to meet her at the hospital in five minutes. I was almost fully dilated and we didn't have time to waste. I begged her to allow me to try for a normal birth, but she insisted it was too risky in a small hospital without the necessary monitors.

The two-minute drive back to my parents' home was agony. I walked bent over into the foyer. I was sure the baby would drop out any second. The telephone rang. It was Clinton. I told him I couldn't really talk as our baby was about to be born. He was calm, but worried. The baby was only due in another three weeks and he wanted to be there for the birth. Although I was in great pain, I remained absolutely calm, sure of God's protection and love.

In hospital I was put on a drip to stop all contractions. Once stable, I was taken to the operating theatre and Christa proceeded with the epidural. Because the labour had progressed so far, she initially wanted to give me a general anaesthetic. I begged for an epidural, held her hands and prayed for her. I asked the Lord to help her and bless the procedure. She sort of looked at me strangely, wondering what the bush had done to me. Her husband, also a doctor, and Dr Willem Schonken assisted.

Christie had donned theatre gear and was allowed to take photographs of the birth. It was only in Bredasdorp that this would be allowed! While they were slicing my belly open, the three doctors were gaily discussing their Christmas party they were having that afternoon. Christa asked my opinion on an ingredient for a salad. I was feeling slightly nauseous and told her I really did not want to talk or think of food right then. These doctors had done so many deliveries and were so capable that they could operate and chat away about other things at the same time.

Soon I heard them talk more seriously. The umbilical cord was wrapped around the baby's neck three times. They severed the cord quickly and I heard my baby girl's first cry. Thank the Lord for the intense pain during my contractions earlier that morning which made me abort the idea of giving birth at home! Thank God also that Christa had insisted on a Caesarian. All had gone well. She was a beautiful, strong and healthy seven pound two ounce baby!

Being a patient in the small Otto du Plessis Hospital in Bredasdorp was wonderful. The personal attention I received was so different to the care in big hospitals. Friends and family popped in regularly. My room was filled with flowers and Gisèle and Michael could see their new sister twice a day. I couldn't wait for Clinton to see our daughter. We still had not decided on a name!

After a couple of days I was discharged from hospital. I was still very sore from the operation and was so grateful for my mother's helping hands. Our baby was so good and content, but coping with three small children all of a sudden proved to be exhausting. Gisèle wanted to help with the baby, but Michael eyed her suspiciously for a while. She was taking up a lot of his mommy's time and he resented that to some degree. I made him sit on the floor and hold her. I told him I needed his help with his baby sister and that went off well. When he saw me breast-feeding her, he asked if he could join in. No problem, I thought. I had enough milk for both. He would often go and check if she was awake so they could feed. Soon the novelty wore off and he was happy to hand over his favourite beverage to his sister. To him that was his biggest contribution towards her health.

Clinton arrived with these words, "Hi my Love. Show me what we have produced!"

He just loved this little bundle that had survived against all odds. We discussed a name for her and eventually settled on Janine. He said he knew a lovely Janine who had good morals, so the name was permitted! Janine lives on a farm in Cradock and is married to Butch Louw. She just laughed when we told her years later how we had decided on a name for our daughter. Janine's second name is Lynette, named after Clinton's mother.

I watched Clinton baby talking Janine. I was amazed at the immediate bond between the two of them. Here was this big, strong, tough man making googly noises to his baby. I felt so wealthy and blessed by the love in our family.

If we, as humans, could feel such love for our children, how much more is God's love for us? How much greater is His ability to care for us and work the best outcome for us when we have repented after having made poor choices. If we could have an inkling of the purity of His love for us, we would not question His motives so readily. We would realize there is no intention to hurt us, only to redeem us.

CHAPTER 18
A BRIGHT NEW DAWN

We returned to Botswana after Christmas to a hearty welcome from our staff. My heart sank as my gaze swept the garden. Most of the shrubs, the lawn and all the flowers had died. Only the hardy stuff survived. I was furious and demanded from Freddie to tell me how this could have happened. The problem was the generator. They were unable to pump water. Clinton wanted to see the animals immediately, but Freddie said they were fine. They had scooped up water from the river and taken it to the camps with the tractor.

My homecoming was spoiled. I was devastated because of my garden. The temperature was above forty-five and my house, without the garden to camouflage it, looked more ugly than ever. The heat, drought and dismal surroundings made me despondent. Only after Gisèle and Michael started chasing each other around on their bicycles and the dogs showed how happy they were to see us again, did my spirit lift a little. I tried to focus on the good things and count my blessings instead of moaning. I tried so hard to thank God for our health and happiness in an effort to rise above our circumstances.

Into Africa

Gobopamang had also had a baby and Anna was wonderful with Janine. Both Michael and Gisèle had learnt to speak Setswana and the staff adored them. Whenever it was necessary for me to discipline them, the staff would hide them or make excuses for them. Batswana were very gentle people and did not believe in hidings.

In an effort to revive my garden I regularly "borrowed" water from the maize land's irrigation system. I could not even deny it, as a distinctive dip in the height of the maize around those two pipelines proved my guilt. Clinton loved a nice garden as much as I did and did not moan too much.

After two months I marveled at the resilience of nature as my garden was looking good again. Plants I was sure had died, came alive again. Julia had given me many slips and seedlings from her garden and I started planting flat out again. Soon I had a garden full of flowers and Clinton had a happy wife again. So many of my plants had come from friends that my garden could tell its own story of friendship. I started doing arrangements to thank my friends who had spoiled me with gifts for Janine's birth. There was no florist in town or fresh flowers for sale. I was inundated by requests for floral arrangements from people who had seen these fresh flowers in town. I started planting more flowers to keep up with the demand. People were ordering coffin sprays, anniversary bouquets, wedding flowers and more. The thought of starting a little business crossed my mind.

Lynley Talbot, our pastor's wife, Lindy Rootsey and Linda Cook came to visit me on the farm. I was so encouraged by them and I related everything that had happened to me. I shared the wonderful miracle of Janine's conception and birth. Because they were mature Christians, they understood exactly where I was spiritually and their support meant so much to me.

I went to church again the following Sunday. I felt the need to be baptized and arranged this with Pastor Rod Talbot for the next Sunday. I knew I was going to be heavily criticized by many of my friends and family who did not agree with adult baptism. They were taught that you were baptized as a baby and that it was sinful to baptized again. But my Bible said that if you believe and confess Jesus as your Saviour, then you should be baptized. A baby can't do either.

Chris Jackson had given Clinton a study Bible. He started reading in order to understand what had happened to me. Because Clinton already had the faith of a child and had experienced miraculous healing as a youngster, it did not take long for him to believe that the Bible was indeed true and powerful.

On 1 April 1990 I was baptized in the Jackson's swimming pool. Hettie attended because she was my friend, but still believed it was wrong. Clinton stood watching quietly from under a tree. I could see he was deep in thought.

When I came out from under the water, something wonderful happened to me. I started speaking in this strange language I did not understand and the most incredible peace surrounded me. Jesus himself was only empowered by the Holy Spirit to work miracles after He had been baptized. Nowhere in the Old or New Testament do I find a single baby baptized. Babies were dedicated to the Lord and the parents promised to raise them in God's ways. Only when they had made a decision for Christ themselves, were they baptized.

Hettie was the first to hug me as I stepped out of the pool. She said she felt touched by God and that something had happened to her. The presence of God was so real and had stirred something inside her.

My focus had shifted away from circumstances and onto God. I saw God's ability and not my inability, His answers and fewer of my questions. I knew I had found something very precious. I had moved into a relationship and out of religion.

A month later Clinton gave his life to the Lord. I never pushed him, just supported him. He had seen the serenity that my relationship with Christ had brought into my life and liked what he saw. My positive attitude to our everyday problems had been an encouragement to him. He knew he needed God's strength and wisdom. We all need that.

Hettie and Clinton were both baptized a couple of months later. We had entered into a relationship with Jesus, which brought inner peace and fulfillment to our lives.

CHAPTER 19
KARIBA

The demand for my floral arrangements increased and I started importing flowers from the market in Johannesburg. Oupa Rahim had a cold room in his butchery next to Hettie's shop. I would put the flowers in buckets of water in the cold room until I did the arrangements. This helped tremendously, but the carting of arrangements from the farm to town proved to be a real test. The staff, who had to hold these arrangements in the moving vehicle, were only too aware of my displeasure should stems be broken before delivery. Eventually I found it very difficult to find anyone to do this job willingly.

I needed premises in town from which to work. The Bosele Hotel had a huge ladies bar, referred to by the locals as the snake pit. This bar was not as popular as the pool bar and I asked the management if I could rent this space. This bar also had a large open-air courtyard where people used to sit and drink around little tables, which would be perfect for a plant nursery. There was plenty of parking just outside the entrance as well. The entire set-up was perfect for what I wanted to do. There was a small kitchen and three Coke fridges where I could keep the fresh flowers as well as a spacious rest room. They agreed to a lease and I started planning my shop!

I had been saving every thebe since I started doing flowers six months before and had enough to pay the rent for the first three months as well as redecorate the place. The Hotel had agreed to paint it out. The most expensive addition would be the shelving. I had ordered two huge steel frames from Tri-3 Engineering. The shelves would be fitted onto them. While we were trying to fit these together, we found that the T-piece on the one frame needed to be bent over for the frame to fit. Trevor and Lesley Frost just happened to walk in at that moment. Trevor was accustomed to making a plan in the bush and quickly climbed up on the ladder. To our astonishment, he bent over the solid iron with his bare hands and the problem was fixed!

Mike Hehir sent down two carpenters and all the wood necessary for the shelving. They worked non-stop for a week and did a wonderful job. When I went to pay him he told me to forget about it. When I insisted, he told me in his Irish accent to get lost in the nicest possible way. I was bowled over at his generosity and found myself with a lump in my throat. No wonder God blessed him so much. Mike did many good deeds nobody ever knew about, but the Lord noticed every one.

While I was waiting for the hotel to finish painting, I made small dried flower bowls and potpourri sachets as well as many other little gift articles to sell in the shop. I had been planting slips in black plastic bags and these plants were looking healthy and good enough to sell. I was so excited about this venture. I knew nothing about business – only that I had to get in more money than I gave out if I wanted to survive.

After heavy rains that lasted for quite some time, our lives were as interesting as ever. The river had come down in flood and subsided again. One Sunday after church I drove home with the children. Clinton was away flying for Trevor Frost.

Our tractor and plough were stuck in the middle of the river in the soaked sand. The only part of the tractor we could see was its cab. It was lying on its chassis and the wheels had just about disappeared under the slosh. Taps had obviously been struggling for a long time to drive it out because it had dug itself deep into the riverbed.

Michael was very upset. This tractor was the most important thing on the farm to him and he was sure it would disappear into the sand completely. He kept on stressing the importance of a rescue mission. Whatever happened, we had to save the tractor.

It was Sunday lunchtime. No workers were around. The river might come down again and wash away our prized possession without which we could not farm at all.

I was angry that he had taken a short cut across the river in the time I was away, instead of driving around the longer but safer way. I got out of the Land Rover, took off my shoes and walked to the tractor. On the opposite side of the river, enjoying a picnic with his family, Manual Batista, a panel beater from Phikwe, came strolling over.

He had witnessed Taps's struggle for the past two hours and was amused at a woman behind the steering wheel of the half-buried monster.

"You can forget about getting it out without the help of earth moving equipment," he said.

Where on earth would I find that on a Sunday afternoon? Dick Smith was away and he was the only person who owned that kind of equipment.

Into Africa

I had to try. Why did these things always happen when Clinton was away? The tyres made no contact with bottom of the dongas they had spun out. The crowd of inquisitives grew and I looked at this mess tiredly.

The task was impossible for me, but possible for God.

"Ok Lord, show me what to do", I asked softly. I knew that He would help me.

I told the crowd that Modimo (God) would help us to get the tractor out. A woman started laughing and said I was mad. Rod had preached on the power of God that morning and I thought this a good opportunity to put my faith to the test.

I asked the men to bring any long piece of sturdy wood they could find along the river. This we thrust down and under the tyres until we had built up a small platform under each tyre. I asked them to shove in extra pieces as I started the tractor, put it into four-wheel drive low range and locked the differential. I put it in first gear and it slowly moved up a little against the branches. Before it rocked back, I shouted for them to force in more wood behind the tyres. This rocking motion and the forcing of more branches in front and at the back of the tyres slowly started producing the desired effect. The tractor was rising and the men kept on putting new grip under the slowly turning wheels. After twenty minutes I drove the tractor out of the slosh, turned it around, hooked the plow and drove out of the riverbed.

I was overcome by the way God had helped me do the seemingly impossible. I stopped the tractor and asked the people who had helped us today. They all stood around, silenced. Taps was the first to speak.

" Modimo, Mma Rice. Only Modimo could do this great thing."

Together we bowed our heads to thank the Lord for his mercy and patience with all of us. God's power was displayed there that day and I thought I would never doubt His ability again.

Our farming venture was not going too well. We realized that the Department of Wildlife could stall the export permits indefinitely. We also knew that the ostrich big shots in South Africa had enormous clout and that they would not relent their efforts to stop live exports from Botswana. They controlled 98% of the international ostrich trade and did not want other countries to farm with live ostriches. Many documents personally handed in to the Dept. of Wildlife simply "got lost" or their receipt was denied.

We couldn't hang in there any longer. We had a family to feed and were forced to think of an alternative plan to survive. Our landlord had also lost faith in the prospect of making money from ostriches and the new deal of P3000 rental per month for the farm was too much for us to make a living there any longer.

We had lost four years of intense work and had to leave without a cent. It was very hard to tell our staff that we no longer had work for them. Admitting defeat after four years of blood, sweat and tears was not easy.

The prospect of my shop now seemed an answer to prayer. Trevor Frost also offered Clinton a job at Longstaff Diamond Drilling Company in Selebi-Phikwe. This job came with a house in town and we could breathe again. Lesley and Mary showed me the house in town and I remember walking through every room, so excited at the prospect of living in a proper, normal brick and mortar home again.

In retrospect, it was a really ugly house, but then it seemed like a palace in comparison to our shack on the farm. Funny how relative everything in life is. After our Kubu trip my shack looked good. It seemed to me your present environment and circumstances can so easily define all other concepts. How fickle human nature seems to be. May be that is why we are warned in the Word to fight it. We readily hide behind our human natures. What exactly is this nature? It is a selfish thing. Something we use as an excuse for all that goes wrong. When we are depressed we quickly find a reason to justify it, instead of fighting it off by focusing on some positive area of our lives. It feeds on ungratefulness. It thrives on self-pity. In short, it makes everyone around you negative and fed-up.

But we have this thing called our "nature" and we cannot ignore it. What can we do, then, to tame it and temper it into an attribute? We all know an undisciplined child is not a pleasure. The same applies to our natures. It takes a great deal of disciplining and hard work to panel beat it into a blessing. It is not pleasant. It hurts like hell. But the fruit of a healthy and positive nature is sweet. It draws people to you. It encourages others who are down. It asks a lot, but gives back even more. As long as the focus is on yourself, you will always feel self-conscious and less than good enough.

I found that while I was focusing on the love and strength of God, I could do all things. As soon as I focused on my circumstances, my ability fluctuated from excellent in good times to very poor in bad times. We all have to face challenges, some harder than others, at certain times of our lives. Life is never going to be fair, because people are not. I wanted a constant to hold on to so that my circumstances would not determine my happiness or lack thereof. That constant became Christ in my life. I found that I was able to be hopeful in dire straits, that my emotions did not entirely dictate my destiny any longer. Whatever came along, I could handle with the help of the Lord. I knew he loved me and would never forsake me. His plans for me are plans to prosper me to give me hope and a future, the Bible says. Why had it taken me so long to figure out this simple truth? It sure made life a lot easier.

Our last evening on the farm was a mixture of relief and nostalgia. We thought of all the good times we had had in this uncivilized piece of Africa, but we were excited about the new challenges that awaited us.

George McAllister had taken our ostriches to Maun. He would take care of them and in return we would get back 10 % of the increase when we were able to farm again.

Seke had put a manager on the farm. After six months there was nothing left and the once productive land had returned to its original state of barren, dusty bush.

Of my once luscious garden there was no trace. Only the very hardy bougainvilleas had managed to survive. I was too saddened by this sight and could not bear going back there.

In town we could use our deep freeze and electrical appliances again. It felt like Christmas opening all the boxes again. We loved having electricity again, but we missed the clean air of the bush. The mine smelter emitted disgusting sulphur fumes that were often carried over the town by the prevailing wind. Most of all we missed our lovely garden and wide lawns. Michael pined for his little bush friends and all the swims they had enjoyed in the river. He missed his tractor most of all. Gisèle had started school at Kopano Junior and had made new friends. Janine was, as usual, happy wherever she found herself.

I could not afford to pay a lawyer to get all the necessary permits and licences for the shop, so I ran around doing it all myself. I was sent back and forth a hundred times. At the council meeting I was asked why I wanted to start this business. To make money, of course! There was a need for a flower shop in town. Flowers meant plants to the Batswana. One member told me that the council already ran a nursery. It took a while to explain what exactly I had in mind for my business. This same gentleman just shook his head and wished me good luck. Six months later this same gentleman came to inspect my shop and was pleasantly surprised. He became a regular customer and admitted that he had had serious doubts when they issued me with a trading permit. He declared my shop the prettiest in town! I also sold gold fish and mudsuckers in small fish tanks.

I decided to call this shop Petals & Pleats. We sold plants, flowers, gifts and clothing (hence the pleats). I ordered an awning above the entrance with Petals & Pleats written on it in an elegant, slanting letter type. I was so pleased with the look of my shop that I couldn't wait to get to work every morning.

I never had a grand opening. I just asked Rod to pray God's blessing over the business before I started trading. I needed the Lord's wisdom and blessing on my first business venture.

Our lives had undergone a fundamental change in a very short period. Clinton started work very early and often worked until long after sunset. I was in the shop from eight to five. We did not have time to sit and watch the sunsets with the children playing around us. At the shop I fabricated a playroom for the children, but they enjoyed feeding the fish more and watering the plants in the nursery. They loved playing in and around the water features in the shop. The parking area became their bicycle-racing track. Anna came along to the shop to look after them and found herself outside chasing after Michael on his bike most of the time.

Janine became Stephanie's most regular customer at her hairdresser salon in the hotel. She would go and visit her and come back with curls or some other crazy hairdo. She was also a good client of the bookshop in the foyer of the hotel – not for books, but candy! Janine loved sweets and the lady at the bookshop simply could not resist her. Janine had grown into this very cute little toddler who stole hearts wherever she went. She was a happy soul who mixed easily with people of all ages. The sparkling pool at the hotel was irresistible to my water babies. They spent many hot afternoons splashing in the baby pool under Anna's watchful eye.

Of all my children Michael missed life on the farm most. He became quiet and withdrawn. I realized that he needed friends of his own age. I took him to Jack and Jill pre-school to see if he would like it. He absolutely loved all the new friends and also enjoyed the classes. Soon Janine wanted to join him, but she was only two and the required age was two and a half. However, she insisted and I checked with Mrs. Austin. She said she would see how the first day went. Instead of playing in the sand pit with the other toddlers, Janine insisted on colouring and cutting out pictures with Michael in the older group. Her hand co-ordination was as good as any and she was allowed to alternate her activities between the toddler group and the pre-school group.

There was one problem. Janine was still breast fed and wanted to know if I could come to school every now and again. I told her that that was not possible. She would then just have to stay with me at the shop. Eventually she had decided that she would simply fill up before and after school, just like the Land Rover. Oh my word! I realized once again. You must think I came from good old dairy stock!

My shop was booming and I was running around like a headless chicken. I was cashier, bookkeeper, manager, florist and saleslady all at once. I was so tired at night that I would simply fall asleep as my head touched the pillow. Clinton said I should think of training people to help me, so that he could at least say good night to me before I fell asleep.

I employed Miriam, a lovely Motswana lady, and taught her to arrange flowers. She had a natural creative streak and soon became an accomplished floral artist. Anna also learnt to arrange flowers and Mazaba did all the banking, post office tasks, watering of the plants and general cleaning. Now there were four of us, and the business ticked over smoothly. Being the only shop where fresh flowers were available, orders from far and wide started pouring in. We had to do flowers for weddings, funerals, special days and many businesses who liked fresh flowers in their foyers. We were expected to deliver the orders and I started looking around for a little panel van. I bought a previously owned Toyota Stallion, wrote the name of my shop on both sides and started delivering in style.

Leslie Proctor saw chance to run a garden service for the shop with a team of local workers. Because of the incredibly hot sun, she decided after a couple of months that she was killing herself and returned to hairdressing. I took over and started a landscaping business instead. I went on a couple of courses in Johannesburg and soon felt ready for this challenge.

We had moved into the fast lane as far as the pace of living in Botswana was concerned. We were now officially in the rat race and we often longed for the peace of the bush. We were however, truly grateful that we had a little money to go away for the odd weekend. The shop enabled us to buy a Volkswagen Microbus. The children loved the space inside this vehicle and they were also able to sleep comfortably during long journeys. We worked very hard, but could see the rewards in terms of comfort.

Clinton was flying a great deal for Trevor. Longstaff had drilling riggs as far away as Zambia and Tanzania. He often flew to Johannesburg to fetch specialized equipment for the diamond drilling machines used by the company.

I managed to employ a really good housekeeper to cook, clean and grocery shop for me at home. I sent her for cooking classes and we were blessed with deliciously wild dishes. One lunch hour she made sandwiches! She had been taught to cut off the crusts and presented these delicate triangles so beautifully that we were all fooled into thinking we had had a healthy meal!

My landscaping took me outdoors and into the scorching sun for long stretches of time. Our first large contract came from Voice of America. They had a radio station 18km outside town from where they broadcast all over Africa. They wanted an enormous area around the new short wave station grassed with fully automatic irrigation. There were three very old, large phoenix canariensis (a hardy type of palm) at their old site and these had to be transplanted at the new station. I knew palms transplant fairly easily because they don't have tap root systems, but I read all information I could get on this process. Trevor rented out his low bed and crane to help load these monsters and transport them to the new VOA site. Clinton and Trevor supervised this long operation patiently and we followed the truck after sunset to lower them into the prepared holes on site. Those palms never took a dip and kept on growing without any loss of leaves. The instant lawn I got from Evergreen Gardens in Johannesburg and André Strydom did the irrigation for me. I had to learn about friction ratios, pipe sizes, pumps and valves. Clinton's expertise was invaluable, as he had had so much experience in the irrigation field. The project was a resounding success and the word spread that there was a landscaper in eastern Botswana.

I stopped for a while to think about the way I simply stepped out into unchartered waters and believed everything was possible. I knew that this new confidence was the result of having faith in my Saviour who guided me every step of the way. I felt such joy and excitement about my business because I believed God's plans for us were plans to prosper us. If only I had dared to trust God like this before!

People, meaning well, would often tell you that something you want to do is impossible. The greatest blessing is not to know that it is impossible, because then you will find ways to make things happen.

Contrary to what I had always thought, this walk with the Lord was super exciting. There were no religious rules to live by, just good old faith in His ability to protect, provide and bless. The fruit of this relationship is sweeter than anything else on earth. He gives so much and only asks our trust. Some of our family and friends thought this relationship we had with Jesus was an understandable crutch after all we had gone through. We knew we had come into a covenant relationship with the only living God. We prayed that they would give the Lord a chance and experience the same peace and joy.

De Beers Mining Company in Serowe contacted me. Their diamond-polishing factory needed a garden quickly for an important function with Ogilvie Thomson of De Beers and the other government dignitaries. Gareth Penny, manager of Teemane Diamond Polishing Company, came to see me and explained what he had in mind. This factory was about two hundred kilometers from Selebi-Phikwe, but in Botswana distance is a fact of life.

I ordered the roll-on lawn from Johannesburg and this time I asked Clinton to help me with the irrigation design. The truck with the lawn arrived late Saturday afternoon and I knew another all-night session awaited me. My team and I had installed the irrigation system by ourselves and I was surprised at how good it felt to start the system and see all the stations spraying perfectly. When the last piece of lawn was laid it was about two in the morning. I had been pulling the concrete roller over the lawn to level the surface and my hands felt raw. I planted colourful petunia seedlings on either side of the paved walkway to add a dash of colour. The final picture was perfect, elegant and simple under the spray lights. We packed up to go home. At half past five that morning we arrived home, exhausted but happy that the project had gone so well.

Two months later I was asked to do all the flowers for the opening of the first diamond-polishing factory in Botswana. I installed a beautiful rock water feature in the foyer and some potted plants to create a cool, refreshing look to counteract the excruciating heat outside.

Dr Quett Masire, president of Botswana, Lady Ruth Khama, Dr Thomson and many cabinet ministers attended the grand opening. The flowers looked gorgeous and Mr. Penny was happy.

At this ceremony I heard the National Anthem of Botswana for the first time. I was touched by the words and music. I was also impressed with the ceremony and the speakers. Botswana is a sparsely populated country within an enormous area of land. At ceremonies like this people mix easily and the usual stiff upper lip protocol is absent. There were a few unobtrusive personal guards around, but no heavy security in your face. I appreciated the safety and security of this country anew.

These words are sung in Tswana, so this English translation is only for your understanding.

BOTSWANA'S NATIONAL ANTHEM

Blessed be this noble land,
Gift to us from God's strong hand,
Heritage our fathers left to us,
May it always be at peace.

Chorus:
Awake, awake, O men, awake!
And women close beside them stand,
Together we'll work and serve
This land, this happy land!

Word of beauty and of fame,
The name Botswana to us came.
Through our unity and harmony,
We'll remain at peace as one.

> Chorus:
> Awake, awake, O men, awake!
> And women close beside them stand,
> Together we'll work and serve
> This land, this happy land!

Our days were hectic, exciting and fulfilling. Financially we could breathe again. The children were busy too – Gisèle with school, Michael and Janine with pre-school and all of them playing hard after school. Gisèle had started ballet lessons with Priscilla Wilson and Michael was being taught to swim in the Bosele Hotel pool.

I was inquisitive about these lessons and wanted to watch, but the swimming coach prohibited this. I hid behind a huge pot plant to peep. Wrong decision! I nearly rushed out to save my child when she, after having playing with him nicely, let go of him. He sank like a stone and I could see the disbelief and shock in his open eyes under the water. He started kicking and soon surfaced, screaming at the top of his voice. She ignored his shouting and starting playing and bouncing him around the water again. He had lost all faith in his coach. She let go of him again and this time he rose quickly, treading water and fighting for his life. She saw me and told me to go away.

"You are drowning him!" I shouted at her. "This lesson is done!"

"He is so relaxed in the water. He's a natural swimmer and if you can control yourself I will drown proof him in another two lessons!" she calmly replied.

I walked off, feeling like the most irresponsible mother on earth. The fact that he was always around the pool in the afternoons and was in danger of drowning because he could not yet swim, made me decide to let her continue. She had taught so many toddlers to swim and came so highly recommended that I forced myself to leave. Back at the shop I howled my eyes out. I could still hear him shout for me in my mind. I was not fit to be called a mother!

After two more lessons, he was able to find the pool's side from any position in the water. When she let go of him, he would simply put his head down and doggy paddle to the side. I was impressed and relieved that he could now help himself, but I still felt terrible about the methods she used to teach him. I couldn't help worrying that he might have built up a fear of water.

However, when he dragged me off to the pool the following week to show me that he could swim, I breathed a sigh of relief! I couldn't get him to get out. He was confident and as happy as a dolphin in the water.

I got a call from Andries, my brother. They were coming to visit. I was quite speechless. In all the years we had lived in Botswana he was always too busy to take time off. Alta, my sister, was driving up with him and his children. My mother was flying up as she said a road trip of 2300km was too much for her. We were all so excited about this visit and we decided to organize a trip up to Kariba with them.

I was blessed to have Antoinette van Zyl working for me in the shop. She was very capable and would take care of things for the week we had planned in Zimbabwe. Longstaff, the company Clinton worked for, generously offered us the use of their houseboat on the lake. This was going to be a wonderful family holiday. Five adults and six children could squeeze into the Microbus easily if we hooked the trailer for the luggage.

Once the crew had arrived, we were entertained by the stories told by Alta and Andries' children concerning their trip up to Botswana. They had traveled the 2300km in approximately nineteen hours, only stopping for fuel and when nature called. Kobus told us that Alta would see a donkey in the road when there was no donkey. She would then shout a warning nobody heeded. I sympathized with her, as my own night sight is not too good either. Everybody agreed she was badly in need of a break.

Listening to Alta's side of the story was as hilarious. She complained bitterly about Andries' lack of responsibility. She hadn't closed an eye throughout the trip! She was too busy fearing for her life as André, then aged nine, sat on his father's lap driving the car at 140km/h with Andries dozing off and snoring loudly!

To top it all, when it was her turn to drive, the music was turned down and the heater put on for the rest to sleep. This induced sleepiness and she had to struggle to stay awake. When she tried to sleep before her shift, the icy Karoo winter wind was allowed free passage through the car and the music was turned up to keep him awake! With these odds against you, you would also see a reindeer or two in the road!!

We were all rolling with laughter as these accusations were flung around, and we felt all the more grateful that they had arrived safely.

At seven the following morning we left for Harare. The trip went well and we arrived after dark at the Cresta Lodge. I could not believe it when the receptionist told me the booking was only for two rooms and not three as I had requested. There were no other rooms available and we eventually booked into the Oasis Hotel in the center of town. Being a Saturday evening, the disco was in full swing and sleep evaded us till three in the morning.

We went to see Aunty Joan, Lyn's sister who was headmistress of Chisipite Junior School. The grounds of both the high and junior schools were beautifully kept and we were all very impressed.

In Harare we stocked up on fresh fruit and vegetables, meat and drinks for our holiday on the houseboat. That evening Alta had crocodile tail and Andries tried the bream, a fresh water fish. Of course he had to remind her that she had eaten something that fed on rotten meat. The kids all pulled faces to show their disgust and Alta just laughed it off. At least she had shown some guts.

As we rounded the bend, the narrow road that led to the jetty at Lake Kariba brought a loud cheer from all of us. It had been a long journey and we all needed the peace and relaxation. There were many houseboats moored in the little bay, some small, some absolutely magnificent. We all tried to spot Voyager first without having a clue what she looked like. We saw two Zimbabwians on the jetty and we were elated when we saw Voyager alongside them. The captain, Finish, and the cook, Godfrey welcomed us happily and carried our luggage and supplies on board. Both were very experienced and Trevor had assured us that we could trust them completely.

Voyager was a wonderful looking vessel and large enough to allow everyone ample space to move around. There were three two-bed cabins, each with an en suite bathroom. On the second deck there were four beds and drop down tarpaulins all around. The children decided that this would be their dormitory. All the decks were enclosed with a meter high reinforced meshing to stop people from accidentally falling overboard. The open deck at the top was perfect for sun tanning. We just knew we were going to have a fantastic time.

We stayed moored for the evening and enjoyed a delicious meal prepared by Godfrey. As we sipped our drinks on deck waiting to be summonsed to dinner, we felt the peace and calm of God's magnificent sunset enveloping us in an atmosphere of complete serenity. We had been transported into another world. After much laughter and fun we retired to our cabins where we were lulled to sleep by the soft sounds of water lapping against the pontoons.

At sunrise we heard Finish starting up the engines and we cruised out into the lake. Godfrey had steaming cups of coffee ready and we were in awe of the beauty surrounding us. Breakfast was another masterpiece by the cook. The wonderful thing was that nobody had to prepare, plan or clean up for meals. At first my mom could not resist conferencing with the cook, but soon she realized there was no need to tell Godfrey what to do or how to do it. It was so good to see her so relaxed and simply enjoying her children and grandchildren without having to do chores.

We cruised peacefully along for most of the day, spotting all kinds of buck, hippo and plenty of crocodiles. At the back of the boat there was a large mesh cage semi submerged in the water where we could splash safely. Later that afternoon we anchored in a small bay where there were no other boats. The setting was exquisite. The late afternoon sun fell gently on the decks and painted the wooden bar in soft shades of golden peach. The waters lapped gently against the boat and the call of the fish eagle reminded us that we were still on earth. I simply don't have words to describe the absolute tranquility, beauty and splendour of the lake. Our holiday on Lake Kariba was like balsam for our souls. As the days passed our baggage of anxieties, exhaustion and cares simply vanished. We could do nothing except enjoy each other's company and the amazing landscape with all its animals ever present on the shores.

A huge African elephant bull strolled down to the water's edge and started drinking of the cool, clear water. He was about twenty meters from us, close enough for us to see his eyelashes. Finish started the little motorboat we had been towing and invited the brave to go closer to the bull. Andries, Clinton, Kobus and André took up the challenge and were so close to the elephant that we held our breath. The old elephant ignored them and continued spraying water over himself. After its ablutions it entertained us with a mock-charge and flapping of its ears to remind us that it was actually still the king around. I laughed as I saw Clinton moving to the further side of the little boat. His respect for an elephant demanded more distance between them!

We enjoyed our dinner on the lower deck amidst a serenade from the frogs. After our meal Finish swung the mounted bulbs out over the dark water around us. Thousands of Capenta fish could be seen gathering beneath the light and a couple of crocodile eyes watched eerily from a distance. This was Africa at its best.

We remained moored for most of the following day and enjoyed fishing and sight seeing from the little out-board motor boat. When we found some hippo and their young in a quiet little bay, Finish asked us to be very quiet near them. We did not want to upset the fiercely protective mothers.

Every day we would move to another beautiful spot and anchor for the night. Finish, an accomplished fisherman, often took the children out on the small boat to fish. They loved these outings and hoped to land the big one the following day. At night they would collapse on their beds after another idyllic day filled with adventure and wild stories about their fishing attempts.

Typical of true Africans, Finish and Godfrey were infinitely patient with the children. Finish never tired of explaining the tricks of navigation to the boys and even allowed them to steer the boat. I saw Michael, donning the captain's cap, smiling smugly behind the steer with only his eyes peeping out from under the cap. My mom did not approve. What if he got head lice?

We anchored near Spurwing Island where Clinton had flown PriceWaterhouse executives some time before. We had to run across the hill to the lodge to replenish some supplies for the houseboat while dodging some buffalo grazing around peacefully

Here Clinton recalled a little episode when he came in to land the Cessna with the executives. Apparently Clint Eastwood was shooting a scene for one of his films here on the island and his jet was coming in fast to land. Clinton was on late finals, but was asked to abort his landing to give way to the jet. He couldn't even see the jet and decided to land first. The jet had to circle a couple of times before it was given clearance to land. The control tower reprimanded Clinton and informed him that he had just caused Clint Eastwood's jet to wait for him to land first. Clinton apologized and decided to wait right there to meet the legend. Clinton shook his hand and introduced himself as Clint Rice. Eastwood looked at him and said in his American accent " Pleased to meet ya, fella. At least we share a good name!"

All too soon our holiday neared its end. On the second last day we had a little scare. We were cruising along and I could not see Janine. She was always with Joanie, but no one had seen her in the past five minutes. I started running around calling for her. We checked all the decks. No Janine! For a minute I was frantic. Had she fallen overboard? Finish stopped the engines and everyone joined the search. At last I found her on the toilet in our cabin. I scolded her for not answering our calls, but she was not concerned about the commotion around her. She just told me to leave her in peace on the toilet! This child of mine was probably the most relaxed human being on God's earth. Nothing upset her, except when she was short on sweet supplies. She joined us afterwards and had no idea of the panic she had caused. Panic did not exist in her make-up. This characteristic was to become her trademark.

We stopped at Chinoyi on our return trip to see the famous Blue Grotto. There were hundreds of steps down to the water and Godfrey's cooking was telling on us. We huffed and puffed all the way up again.

When we arrived at Chegutu, formerly Hartley, we asked for directions to Montebello where my father had farmed and built his first house. This was a journey down memory lane for my mother and she recognized several farms as we drove along. After an extensive search for the farmhouse, we located the spot, but found only ruins where their home had been. We were extremely disappointed and drove back in silence. The house had been destroyed during the civil war that crippled this beautiful country.

Cecile De Neuilly-Rice

On our crossing the border between Botswana and Zimbabwe, we felt flat. We had enjoyed our holiday tremendously and didn't feel ready for the hard work and long hours that awaited us back home.

CHAPTER 20
PETALS AND PLEATS

Gisèle was doing well at school and had made many new friends. Michael and Janine both attended Jack-and-Jill Nursery School with great enthusiasm. Michael did the pre-primary course and Janine joined the colouring and cutting activities. Her great friend was Lebohang Matsepe, whose mother was a Motswana doctor and father a German. These two little girls were inseparable and always played either at the shop or at Lebo's house every afternoon. They always hugged and kissed each other like long lost friends.

A repeat of this scene caused quite a commotion a year later at the Waterfront in Cape Town. While visiting the family in the Cape, we were strolling along past the trapeze artists doing their stunts. Along came the Matsepe family and Janine and Lebo spotted each other first. They shrieked with delight, ran to each other and hugged and kissed. This was in the time of apartheid in South Africa in 1992. The New South Africa had not yet been born and the stares from bemused onlookers were hilarious, especially when we all exchanged hugs. We had a hard time getting the two friends to let go of each other.

Gigi had always passed on her children's clothes to my kids. She bought at expensive stores and these items looked like new when my children inherited them. Gus, Gigi, Kate, Alice and James waited for us to meet them at the waterfront.

As we walked towards them Alice exclaimed, "Look, here come our clothes!" That brought the house down. We laughed about this for a very long time. Alice does not mince her words and we all love her for her sparkling nature.

Back in Selebi-Phikwe we were suffering under a blanket of sulphur emitted from the copper smelter. It was hard to think such pollution possible in the midst of the bush. I wondered why the smelter had not been built on the other side of town for the prevailing wind to clean up. Some days one could taste acid on one's tongue.

Petals and Pleats was a very lucrative little business. Whenever I had to take an important decision, I was guided by the Lord's peace or lack thereof.

Gareth Penny put the Woodfords in contact with me to redesign their English garden in Serowe. This project would be Bill's birthday gift to his wife Paddy. Their home was beautifully furnished with antiques and their hospitality was wonderful. I enjoyed re-doing the garden and felt blessed by this new friendship. Woodfords on the Mall, their business in Serowe, also received a little face-lift with a fountain I installed. Paddy opened a section where she sold seedlings and other gardening items, much to the delight of the local gardeners in Serowe.

The next invitation came from the Francistown Garden Club. They wanted me to speak on indoor and outdoor water features. I was thrilled and started gathering all kinds of visual aids and notes for this talk.

Into Africa

Two days before the event, I tore one of my soft contact lenses. This was very worrying as I am shortsighted and shouldn't drive without my lenses. It was impossible to wear only one lens and I felt extremely unfit behind a steering wheel. I ordered new lenses from South Africa, which could take up to twelve days to arrive. I could not possibly cancel my talk in Francistown and decided to use Michael's eyes instead.

Francistown was a good hour and a half away from Selebi-Phikwe. What I did would have freaked out Gigi completely. Michael stood next to me and warned me of as much danger as a four and a half year old was capable of. I stressed the importance of his job and he took it very seriously. He would warn me when he spotted donkeys, goats or anything else that could run across the road in front of us. I drove very slowly and the trip took us much longer, but we arrived safely. During the talk I actually enjoyed not being able to see individual facial expressions too clearly. I rambled on happily pretending everyone hung on to my lips.

The Francistown ladies were quite different from the Phikwe crowd. Most of them had lived there for very long and their gardening objectives were more permanent. They were prepared to invest heavily in their gardens which were their only refuge from the dusty landscape of Botswana Their families were mostly involved in their own businesses. Francistown is perfectly situated for trading on the main North-South route through Botswana and it is a popular place to overnight and recharge the batteries. It is also much bigger than Selebi-Phikwe. This garden club was very active and the ladies knew their plants. I had a wonderful time with them and was invited to speak to them on a number of occasions after that.

The trip home was another challenge as it was becoming dark. I gave Michael a can of coke to keep him alert. I did not usually allow my children fizzy drinks and he felt rather grown-up to be in charge of my driving whilst sipping his adult drink! With a great deal of grace from God and Michael's careful attention to danger, we made it home safely.

I loved doing flowers for weddings and other functions. My mom-in-law had taught me the basics and I learned more as time passed. On her visits, which often coincided with big functions or funerals, she would throw in her weight and help. I learnt so much about business from her as well as the finer points of floral art.

Because of the arid surroundings, people particularly liked tropical plants like palms, which did well in this frost-free climate. Somehow these plants were out of place in Botswana, but the atmosphere they created in gardens made their owners feel they were in a different world far removed from the dusty African bush.

It was time for me to fetch stock in South Africa and I took Gisèle with me for a dental appointment in Pietersburg. We left early in the morning in the Microbus on the dirt road to the Zanzibar Border Post. This road was, as usual, in a state of disrepair, pot holed and corrugated. I told Gisele to put on her safety belt, something we did not always do. As we rounded a bend, I felt the vehicle losing traction and I did the wrong thing instinctively. I slammed on brakes. I could hear Clinton's warning in my mind. Don't brake around a corner on a dirt road! Too late I tried to correct my folly and the next instant we were rolling over. After two rolls the Combi stopped on its wheels. I was stunned. It had all happened so fast. I checked on Gisèle who was still sitting in her seat, white and shocked. The windscreen had popped out and the air conditioner was still blowing air onto my pale face.

Having watched too many movies where the vehicle explodes after a crash, my first thought was to get her out of the car. I unbuckled us and forced the door open. As we stood alongside the badly damaged Microbus I realized that we could so easily have been killed. Shock made me nauseous and I started shaking uncontrollably. We were both all right. Gisèle had a little cut on

Into Africa

her wrist, but was unharmed otherwise. I dropped to me knees in the dust and thanked God for sparing our lives. I should have given myself a slap for driving like an idiot.

I started collecting the contents of my purse that had been scattered all over. A truck stopped and I asked the driver to phone Clinton from the next village. I thought I was calm and in control again. Soon another car stopped. It was Plum Graham, the manager of Fairways. He rushed over to us and I found myself bursting into sobs. He then organized for the Combi to be moved off the road and took us twenty kilometers down the road to Backline Trading Store, which belonged to Hettie's mother, Rosy van Niekerk. From there he phoned Clinton at work.

When Clinton arrived and saw for himself we were fine he smiled that typical little smile that always worked its charm, and called me Crash Flash. I wanted to hug him and smack him at the same time. He held us both and praised God for His protection. His amused grin on the way home reminded me of the many times I had told him to drive slowly on the dirt roads. I was always lecturing him on his fast driving and here I was, the victim of my own reckless driving.

The Combi had been brought back to our house. Michael took one look at it and said I should not drive without his help again. One look from me stopped further suggestions from him. The next morning Clinton drove it to the panel beater in peak hour traffic. The sight of this sad looking crab-like vehicle attracted much attention and another flood of phone calls from friends resulted.

At the shop Miriam insisted on doing all the arrangements for the day, as I should not stand up, she said. I should actually be in bed making sure I didn't have internal injuries, she advised. The only injury was to my pride, I thought.

Antoinette insisted that she could handle everything for the day and I went home to recover from emotional exhaustion. Rod and

Lynley came to see us. They prayed that Gisèle and I would not suffer from fear after the accident and I knew I was going to be fine. What a relief to have someone as awesome as God to wipe away fear and replace it with renewed confidence.

CHAPTER 21
FREE FROM FEAR

I had been afforded the privilege of a panoramic exposure to the concept of fear.

Fear has many names and many faces, some very distinct, like a hairy spider, some more vague like a gnawing anxiety. Indistinctly defined fears are more difficult to deal with, like a faceless enemy whose course is hard to predict.

I have learnt that any decision based on fear is usually the wrong one. Knowledge can curb fear to an extent. It is the unknown that most frightens us and an understanding of the thing you fear helps you to deal with it more ably.

In South Africa fear of Black domination has been the underlying reason for many political decisions. The white man fears that the black man will destroy his culture and religion and the black man regards the white man with suspicion because of the fear of oppression. The lack of understanding one another's cultures and norms have caused untold casualties on both sides.

In Botswana there is very little racial animosity. As opposed to "Unity is Strength" (the South African motto), Botswana's strength lies in its diversity. The whites comprise Europeans, Asians, South Americans, North Americans and other white Africans. These different groups were so busy checking out one another that the blacks were having a break for a change. The Bamangwato is by far the majority and smaller ethnic groups have happily integrated with them. Imagine if all the colours in South Africa could intermarry and create a whole new rainbow nation where nobody could be classified according to race or culture. My mother would faint when she reads this.

I have had to curb my fear of spiders. I still don't like them, but I have learnt to understand their role in ecology and even that little knowledge has been helpful in reducing my fear.

I also found that this same principle could be applied to different spheres of life. My background dictated certain standards of living and social norms that form the basis of my culture. Now I had been placed in a society that did not necessarily share those norms. The natural reaction is reservation and distrust, fear in yet another form. Fear of rejection is possibly the most ardent form of fear in humans. Many people choose not be become involved in a relationship because that means vulnerability to rejection and hurt. People's behaviour can be directly linked to their fear of rejection. We are social beings with a pack instinct and we want to conform and be part of the group.

I knew a wealthy lady in Phikwe who can be used as a prime example. She was raised by her grandmother and felt her mother had rejected her. This fear of being rejected again made her extremely jealous of any woman who had a conversation with her husband. She is very insecure in her friendships with others and always drops names to impress them. She doesn't even realize that she feels so inadequate. She needs constant approval and fishes for compliments and little signs of acceptance all the time. She talks about her money frequently and tries to buy people's favour by lavishly entertaining them to dinner parties. She loved talking about her acquaintances' titles and qualifications. The more she spoke, the more people of integrity frowned upon her background. The saddest part is that she is actually a good-looking, charming person, who didn't need other's credentials to be accepted.

People like being around others who are comfortable in their own skins. They feel at ease and are encouraged to just be themselves. Because her crutches were money and prestige, both very removable assets, she had no permanent platform from which to project her own identity. She needed to believe that God loves her unconditionally and that her true identity can only be found in Him who is the same yesterday, today and tomorrow. We should all worry more about what God thinks of our actions than what people think of us. The Lord is quicker to forgive, kinder in His assessment and far more loyal than any friend on earth.

Scripture tells us that God's perfect love drives away all fear. The greater our revelation of God's immense love for us, the less fear we will have to cope with. We will be able to focus on His ability to help, rather than the size of our obstacle. Stress is the number one killer of humanity. Stress is fear and it is also the opposite of faith. Faith is believing that help is on its way. Stress is believing that disaster is more probable.

A study has proven that most things we fear never actually happen to us. Fear is time consuming and robs us of our health and joy.

There is only one way to conquer fear and that is by faith; faith in God's ability and willingness to help and protect, which is the same as believing that nothing can separate you from His loving care. Of course, as in all things, it remains a choice that you have to make every day. Fear is the weapon of the enemy we have to face very often. It helps to recognize your enemy, so that you can slay it with the truth from the Word of God.

Good choices are made when you have good information, a good knowledge of God's Word to guide you into the truth that will set you free from fear. Whenever I am facing a difficulty I quote these scriptures to calm me down and give me courage.

"Greater is He who lives in me than he who is in the world."
"I can do all things through Christ who strengthens me."
"Nothing can pluck me from God's hand."
"Do not worry about anything; instead pray about everything."
"God's plans for me are plans to prosper me, not to harm me."
"Faith is the substance of things hoped for, the evidence of things not seen."
"God's perfect love drives away all fear."

We know the Lord's love for us can never change. It consolidates our position in Christ and gives us the freedom to live a victorious life. You cannot be a blessing to someone else if you are fearful and negative. Fear diminishes acumen, that ability of discernment necessary for keen insight into a situation.

The problem with Christianity is that people look at Christians instead of at Christ. They are put off Christianity because of the behaviour of Christians. Christianity is a relationship, not a religion. God created man to have a relationship with Him. In a love relationship there is laughter, fun, honesty, forgiveness and joy. There are also times of anger and frustration, but this is sorted out because of a deep caring for each other. You love someone because of the trust and respect you have for him, not because you fear retribution. Christ is a person who loves us and who doesn't change his mind about us. There is nothing you can do to diminish His love for you. You can, however, choose to reject His blessings and protection, but His love remains constant.

The greatest lie about God is that everything that happens is His will. He tells us not to kill each other and we do. He tells us not to steal and we do. If someone dies we blame God. If someone is sick we blame God's will. Often you hear preachers saying that we have to accept God's will when there is a tragedy. Sure, He knows everything, but we still have a choice. How can you expect a person to love and trust a God who simply murderers your loved ones? He came to save, not to destroy.

"But He allowed it to happen!" we often argue. He has given us freedom of choice, something He will never take back, and we live with the consequences of our choices. He says that we must choose life, not death. We are human and make mistakes all the time. Our greatest fight should be against our own mindsets, our own selfishness and greed. We have a responsibility too, but it is so much easier to shift blame onto God. In the process we alienate good people from a loving God, because we cause them to believe God is the author of disaster.

Of course, your philosophy of life and death is determined by what you believe. If you believe that the Bible is the Word of God, then you will also believe that all good things come from Him. He is not the enemy. He is a loving Father who wants to bless, heal, protect and guide. He has given us everything we need to overcome adversity, but we have to apply it. He says we will all face difficulty in this life, but we are the heirs of His amazing grace, which is enough to help us win every battle. God is never glorified by murder, sickness or tragedies that are blamed on Him.

As the shepherd of His flock He walks in front and leads us. He does not chase us from behind. He never forces us to follow Him, but draws us closer by His Spirit of love in the hope that we will enter into a relationship with Him.

The choice remains ours.

CHAPTER 22
TURNING SOUTH

Apart from the Toyota Stallion, our delivery van, I had no other transport. The insurance had written off the Microbus and paid out.

I found a very comfortable car with low mileage at a good price. Unfortunately it was a rather flashy car and people started criticizing my spending money on a Mercedes Benz. I was a little surprised at this. I learnt some more about people and decided that it was not my problem. I felt so blessed and grateful for this car and I was not going to allow others to make me feel guilty. My reaction is still my choice and I chose gratitude instead of condemnation.

That Sunday in church I really enjoyed the praise and worship. Lynley played the guitar and the congregation sang along happily. The presence of God was so strong in the school hall, where we had church. Clinton had committed his life to the Lord and enjoyed church. He did complain about singing the same song over and over. He said God was not deaf and had heard him the first time. Jesus had become Clinton's friend and he had a very practical, honest relationship with his Saviour.

Every Tuesday evening we had a cell gathering at Rod and Lynley's house. Here everybody shared their blessings and concerns. We became like a family. Clinton would speak his mind and often had people gaping. He just was not going to conform for the sake of sounding spiritual. He questioned, found answers in the Word and believed. If God said it, that settled it for him.

In many ways Clinton was the most honest Christian I ever knew. He never tried to impress others by being a good Christian. He was good to people because he enjoyed giving of himself and liked company. When the Springboks and the Kiwis played rugby against each other the comments between Rod and Clinton had us all in fits of laughter. Rod supported New Zealand and Clinton South Africa.

Longstaff had suspended all exploration drilling projects for BCL. There was talk of the mine closing down. Copper prices were down and the mine was operating at a loss. Clinton's two-year contract with Longstaff was nearing its end and we had to think ahead. I wanted Clinton to join Petals and Pleats to boost our irrigation section, but he had other plans.

A South African syndicate wanted to buy Clinton's ostriches to farm with them in the Tuli Block. Clinton found out that the Department of Wildlife had eventually agreed to allow exports from Botswana. This was what he had been waiting for. He decided to farm with his own ostriches and export them himself.

We would hire a farm in the Tuli Block and go farming again. This was great news for the kids who loved life in the bush. However, the children were at school in Selebi-Phikwe and my shop was doing well. We put our heads together and decided we would sell Petals and Pleats and I would home school my children on the farm, which was 140km from Selebi-Phikwe. There was no way we would live apart.

Gisèle had been attending ballet classes with Cilla Wilson for two years. Cilla was interested in buying the shop and I set up a meeting with the Wilsons and my auditors. A price was agreed upon and we started negotiations with Jannie Brink to hire a section of his farm, Peg's Valley, in the Tuli Block.

Selling my shop was emotional for me, but I had been working so hard and longed for some quality time with my family again. Cilla wanted to keep the staff and I was grateful that these dear ladies would not lose their jobs.

Every time we went down to the farm, we would take along as much as we could in the Toyota. The farmhouse was enormous, but in need of some painting and repairs. There were four huge bedrooms, each with its en suite bathroom. It had been built as a hunting lodge a long time ago. The kitchen was a 12m x 8m hall with an enormous wooden table in the center. There was a big swimming pool in a bad state of disrepair, but with the help of Nigel Bellamy and Andre Campbell we fixed it with nito-seal and it never leaked again.

Aunty Joan Howard went to see Mr. Chikari at the Government Correspondence School in Harare and organized for me to join their correspondence school system. She said the standard was excellent and that put my mind at ease. All seemed set and we were ready to embark on yet another adventure.

Marc, Clinton's brother, Helene and their two children, Tracey and Michael, came to visit us. We were expecting Andries and his children as well and decided to take a trip to the Victoria Falls together. We would travel in three cars in convoy. A large family gathering like this was rare and we looked forward to a very special time together. The children made turns in all the cars and we caught up on all their news en route to the Victoria Falls.

Janine, being the youngest, was also the most inquisitive and least inhibited. Andries recalled an awkward silence in their car after a rather personal question posed by her. In our home it was not strange to see Clinton walking to and from a shower in the nude. In fact, we were a bit of a nudist colony at home. I think the unbearable heat in Botswana had pushed us over the edge of normal behaviour. I remember my mom once asking Clinton if it was true that he walked around naked at home. She had told my kids to put on their nightgowns when they ran naked from the shower to the bedroom and they were surprised that she had even noticed. This was when they had told her that going stark naked was quite the norm in our home.

Clinton's answer had her giggling all day. "Of course that's true. Advertising pays!"

Janine wanted to know if the males in Andries's family had also been circumcised! She never got an answer, but caused a roar of laughter when this story was told later. My mom would have been shocked.

We stayed in a chalet at the Safari Lodge near the Vic Falls. It was a bit of a squeeze to fit in all the children and Gisèle and Tracey opted to make their beds in the spacious closet. Marc and Helène's son, Michael, entertained us by singing the new South African Rainbow Nations' song "Shosholoza" with all the energy he could muster.

Apart from the incredible magnitude of the cascading water, we loved the little colony of mongooses on the lawn in front of the chalet. They had become used to tourists feeding them and, perched upright in anticipation of breakfast morsels, we happily obliged by giving them whole raw eggs. The way they cracked open these eggs was very interesting. They would stand on their hind legs, grip the eggs with their front paws while pointing their behinds at a rock, and fling the eggs backwards underneath their little bodies to hit the rock and crack open. The smell of an egg caused the same reaction from a mongoose as a bleeding carcass would from a lion.

At the grand old Victoria Falls Hotel Helène and I wandered around admiring its old world splendour, wondering if we would ever be able to afford a stay in such a luxurious place.

We had spent a week of absolute bliss together. For a while we were far removed from the pressures of everyday life. The happy memories made during our holiday together would serve to strengthen the healthy bond that had always existed between us.

CHAPTER 23
TULI BLOCK DAYS

Clinton started erecting the electric fencing around the 120 hectares of quarantine area in which the ostriches were to be kept. The regulations for export were very strict and the specifications from the USDA explicit. That meant double fencing three meters apart all around. No poultry was allowed within a radius of three kilometers of this area. This was to prevent disease spreading to the export birds. The incubator room and chick-runs were to be kept sanitized and free of droppings at all times. Anyone entering the incubating area had to step into a shallow trough filled with a strong disinfectant.

The horrendous Zanzibar dirt road had caused us many punctures, but eventually all our belongings were safely in the old farmhouse. I started crack filling and painting like a possessed person. We started preparing our schoolroom for the following year.

There was time again to bake cookies for the children and to play with them in the mud. How we just loved having time for one another again. I could be a mommy again and Clinton was at home every day. We all loved our new home and life on the farm.

One Saturday afternoon we were cooling off in the pool when Clinton arrived with a tiny vervet monkey clinging to his neck. Its mother had been killed and the little orphan became our pet. Everyone fought for BB's attention and affection. BB stood for Blue Balls. When we realized much later that it was a female, we decided BB could also stand for Bush Beauty.

This little creature brought much joy to the children. Janine would push her around in her doll's perambulator and pretend it was her baby. It was hilarious to watch BB eat porridge. She would stuff her cheeks so full that I thought the two pouches would burst open. Typical monkey, she was very inquisitive and insisted on tasting whatever we were eating or drinking. Clinton had a cup of tea and BB hung onto his arm to see what was inside the cup. She stuck her head in the cup and was shocked at the heat. This did not deter her for long and she wanted more. Clinton added a little milk to cool it down and BB hung on to the rim of the cup for dear life. We took a video of her hanging from the rim with her head stuck in the cup.

As she grew older she became very demanding of my attention. Jealousy reared its ugly head and she resented Janine as my baby. She would wait for Janine to sit on the toilet before she launched her attack. The clever monkey knew she was the proverbial sitting duck there. BB would jump up on her lap, pretend to play and then quickly try to bite her on the cheek. Janine knew what BB was up to and the poor monkey would, more often than not, receive a shove that would land her on the floor. Clinton did not like this at all and said we would have to give her away before she scarred his daughter's face. The kids did not want to lose her and simply denied that she had bitten them even if the evidence was quite obvious.

When school started BB had to be banned from the classroom. She often grabbed Michael's pencil and jumped on top of the highest shelf where she would chew it to pieces while spitting the remnants down on the children. Michael welcomed these interruptions, but I could not have it any longer.

Every two weeks their work was sent off to Mrs. June Rule in Harare who kept a close eye on their progress. She was most impressed with the children and commended them on their work.

Clinton started working on their swimming techniques and we played table tennis, hockey and soccer with them on the lawn.

At school Clinton had represented Eastern Province in five different sports – swimming, rugby, athletics, diving and gymnastics, so he was more than qualified to show them the ropes. The children were developing beautifully academically, physically and emotionally. We were having the time of our lives on the farm. At least we had electricity here and I could boil water in a kettle and cook on a stove.

The children played under the enormous old Scotia tree in the afternoons. They built farms in the dirt, complete with bridges over streams and camps for their stock. They traded and visited one another's "homes". Janine was sent to fetch cold drinks and home-made biscuits from my kitchen in exchange for scraps of junk the other two convinced her could be used to decorate her "yard".

They would sometimes go to the veld with one of the staff, who taught them which wild berries were edible. They also learnt to track the elephants and I would be presented with a ball of elephant dung, which would be pulled apart to show me what the beast had had for lunch the previous day. Elephant dung is very coarse, contains poorly digested roughage and does not smell badly at all.

Something interesting always happened in the Tuli Block and Clinton was never far from the action. He overturned the double cab on a wet and slippery dirt road en route to Phikwe. Windscreens seem to pop out easily on the Zanzibar road. He got the pick-up back on its wheels again and came home, as it was illegal, even in Botswana, to drive around without a windscreen. The roof was dented badly but the rest looked all right and we drove with it for another two weeks before the panel beater had time to fix it. During these two weeks I had to wear ski goggles to prevent insects from flying into my eyes.

The children and I drove to Terrafou, a farm about eleven kilometers from Peg's Valley, to collect something. It started drizzling and the children ducked for cover behind the front seat. They were giggling at my ski goggles and the sight I must have looked. Soon the rain came down heavier and the drops stung my face. There was no cloth in the vehicle to wipe off the raindrops on the goggles and I struggled to see. I asked the kids to find anything that I could use. My bush babies quickly made a plan and Gisèle donated her panties for the job. She stood behind me and wiped the lenses every couple of seconds to clear the now pouring rain as best she could.

A couple of kilometers further we hit an impala standing in the road. Fortunately we were going very slowly and instead of being flung out the open windscreen, the children only fell forward against the back of the front seat and I felt the thud of their collective impact behind me. I slammed on brakes (I'll never learn) and the kids did a second landing behind the seat. The poor impala lay in the middle of the road without moving, but still breathing normally. I was convinced it was simply knocked out cold and would survive. There was no blood or sign of injury and I gently moved it off the road. On our way back we would check it out again.

When I told the farmer at Terrafou, he laughed so loudly that I looked around to see who else found this funny. He said that the buck's back or neck had most probably been broken. The first passing donkey cart would have picked up the buck. It was probably becoming supper to some poor family as we spoke.

That evening I reminisced about the past seven years in this country. I found it hard to stop a feeble smile. How was it possible that our adventure never seemed to end? There was always something out of the ordinary happening. The craziest thing was that these happenings were seen as normal here.

Theunis Klopper, a very good friend of ours, was driving us in the still damaged double cab. En route, we were stopped by the police at Baines Drift Police Station. The policeman took one look at this huge guy with the ski goggles behind the steering wheel of a very crinkle-cut vehicle and decided this combination was definitely not roadworthy. While the officer was complaining bitterly, Theunis tried hard not to smile. He hooted, indicated both ways, braked and put the lights on to show everything that needed to work, worked perfectly.

"Eish, Sa. This vehicle is not good."

"Do you allow donkey carts on this road?" Theunis enquired of the man.

"Yes, sah, we du, but.."

"Is this vehicle no better than a donkey cart, officer? I will tell Mr Rice what you think of his car," Theunis retorted seriously.

At this stage the officer simply wanted to make the problem disappear and opened the gate to allow us through. He muttered, " Auk!…Lekgoa!" (These white men!)

BB had become too aggressive and we sadly parted with our monkey. Koffie and Ansie Versveld were two of our good friends who adored animals. They were keen to take BB. We knew BB would be cared for and loved in their home. They also had a pet banded mongoose called Kiri whom BB immediately adopted as her baby. BB grabbed her "baby" and climbed high up in a tree. We were worried that she would drop Kiri to her death, but she clung onto her precious cargo and eventually brought it down again.

At night the monkey and the mongoose shared a bed on a pillow in a box. Kiri accepted the flea search from her adopted mother because she had no choice. After the ablutions, BB would carry Kiri off to bed and cover them both with the blanket. The monkey held Kiri close to her and dozed off. Kiri wasn't ready for bed and crept out. As soon as BB saw Kiri had gone, she got up, half asleep, and went off to find her. She carried Kiri off to bed again and covered them both with the blanket again. This behaviour became a ritual and caused Ansie and Koffie much amusement. Once BB helped Kiri find some earthworms in the soil. The only gratitude she got from the mongoose was a bloody finger. Kiri was not going to share her lunch with anyone.

When the Versvelds left, Daan and Julia rehabilitated BB into the wild. Kiri was given to us. The children adored her and watched her dig up spiders, put her foot on her prey while breaking off the legs and devouring it like a pie.

The children all wanted Kiri to sleep with them until they discovered that she marked her territory by urinating in her sleeping place. Kiri was given her own blanket and box where she could perfume it to her liking.

Kiri and Tao, our Boer Bull puppy, became good friends. The two of them slept close together and played all day long. When Kiri came into season the first time, she kept on shoving her behind under Tao's nose. He could not understand what she wanted.

During school time she would climb into Michael's shirt and snuggle up against the warmth of his tummy. Whenever he moved and disturbed her peace, she would shriek and could only be settled down with a snack of some sort. Michael, who much preferred the outdoors, would often deliberately disturb her to gain some playing time outside.

To complete our circus, Hettie gave the kids a male and female rabbit. As you well know these animals breed fast and soon there were quite a few rabbits around chewing away at my vegetables and garden. I was beyond the point of fighting nature and simply planted enough for the rabbits as well.

Janine has always been very ticklish. I once saw her lying flat in the rabbit cage with baby bunnies running all over her. Some of them got burrowing in her neck and she screamed with delight as their little noses tickled her.

Henroux Schoeler, a school friend of Michael's, came to spend a month with us on the farm. His mom and her husband were about to leave for the United Arab Emirates where Louise's husband was to start a new project for his company. Henroux preferred staying in Africa until his parents had sorted out their new home. He joined our school and provided Michael with the necessary challenge to try his best.

After school they would play under the tree and build more camps and imposing entrances to their farms. Louise had sent along a complete collection of plastic farm animals for them to play with. Gisèle and Janine were allowed to decorate their yards with blooms from my garden. Michael and Henroux ploughed their lands with their tractors, bought and sold sheep from each other and complained of the drought. Tiny bridges over steams were redesigned and reinforced until their laden trailers could cross without falling through into the river. Michael laughed until tears rolled down his cheeks when Henroux's first bridge gave way and his trailer and sheep fell out into the stream. Henroux packed up laughing too and together they fixed the bridge. When Henroux wanted to put the sheep back into the camp, Michael reminded him that they had all drowned and should rather be taken to the abattoir to be slaughtered, or even better, be handed over to him to nurse back to life and then join his flock.

When I took them tea and biscuits I had to see every new addition to their farms. More often than not, I ended up playing with them and enjoying their make-believe world more than they realized.

The children played hard, but also fought hard. Gisèle and Michael could really have a go at each other. She would attack like a windmill with arms and legs swinging and kicking. Michael would choose a target and zoom in on it until he had delivered a decent blow that would either end the fight or cause a more severe attack from his sister. He was not allowed to hit her on the boobs and she was not allowed to kick him between the legs. If one cried, both were given a hiding. We did not encourage fighting at all, but it was going to happen and there had to be rules at least.

"What boobs? I can't hit something that does not even exist!" he complained.

"They are there, you silly! They just haven't come out yet!" she lashed back.

Being a woman, playing dirty was second nature. She would sometimes run to Clinton and accuse Michael of having hit her there. He would take his hiding, but would pay her back by pretending to curl up in pain after a blow to the family jewels. They were quick to forget and forgive and never tired of each other's company. Janine was supposed to be neutral, but sometimes Gisèle would pick her up and order her to kick like mad. She would then charge at Michael with Janine like a battering ram held in front of her.

I believe that children who fight and sort out themselves are often very close when they grow up. This has proved to be so true in my children's case. Today they stick together and protect one another. There are no unresolved issues between them. They don't bear grudges because they deal with things as they come up. Sometimes I think they are too direct with one another, but it seems to work for them. Michael is quick to point out weight gain on his sisters and Gisèle would lash back by calling his lips Congo smackers. Janine was teased constantly for buying rubbish. I reminded them of their conning her into doing chores for them and then rewarding her with their discarded trash.

The two of them decided to teach Janine to roller skate. What a sight she looked with a pillow tied to her backside and a crash helmet on her head! They flanked her and held her hands to stabilize her. It did not take long before she could skate down the length of the enormous verandah by herself.

The girls loved dressing up in my clothes and acting out scenes from videos they had watched. Michael was never an enthusiastic member of these concerts and caused more havoc than anything else. Gisèle always directed the plays and was very sure of what she wanted and how things should be done. Because of Janine's natural gymnastics ability, she was always required to dance, split or do handstands during scenes. Her bum was up in the air more often than her head.

In one scene Michael was required to use his clap gun. Gisèle was taking too long organizing some décor and he started looking elsewhere for something to shoot. He found a cricket on the carpet and started shooting at it. The poor insect jumped a record distance with Michael hot in pursuit. After another couple of shots the cricket must have died of fright. He was pleased to announce that he had saved my carpet from the cricket that would most certainly have eaten a hole in it. Gisèle restored order and continued barking out orders for the following scene. Before Michael could cause a riot, I arrived with some cold drinks and biltong to give the crew a welcome breather.

Before lunch one day, Clinton walked in with his shorts in tatters. A male ostrich had kicked him and he managed to turn just in time to save his manhood. The blow hit him on the hip and half tore his pants off his body. A big bruise and scratch marks indicated the severity of the kick.

"I managed to grab my high-stepping dance partner by its head and hold it down until I reached the gate! Thank goodness I saved my jewels, otherwise my voice would have gone up a couple of octaves!" This man was simply amazing. He could have been killed and here he was joking about it all. His limp told a different story, though.

After a trip to town to stock up on supplies, we arrived home to a very upset housekeeper. Florah told us of a youngster who had come to visit someone on the farm. Kiri ran out to him and he thought it was a rabid wild mongoose trying to bite him. He had killed Kiri in self-defense.

I was absolutely furious and wanted to see the young man immediately. Luckily for him, he had left straight after the horrible deed when Florah told him it was our favourite pet.

We all cried for our beloved Kiri and Clinton had his hands full trying to restore peace at home. The children were ready to avenge Kiri's murder and had already embarked on a plan to find the little sh.t and kill him too. It took a great deal of convincing to get them to put down the whip, hockey stick and clap-gun that they were going to use to kill the culprit.

We took a short break and went to visit Ouma Sykes in Zimbabwe. She was deep in her nineties and very frail. We knew this would be a final visit to Clinton's grandmother. Janine's only recollection of this visit was of Ouma Kathleen's teeth in a jar on the shelf. She found it fascinating that teeth could be taken out of your mouth and be put back again. No tooth fairy would fall for that one!

We stayed with Malcolm Duncan, Clinton's cousin, and his wife Agnes. Agnes got me a Jack Russell puppy and went to huge trouble to obtain an international removal permit from the vet. We called the puppy Mally after Malcolm.

Mally was a good looking little dog with a slight underbite that caused problems for him when he tried to catch a flea on himself. Gisèle made sure he was bathed regularly to keep him flea-free.

Tao (Tswana for Lion) got on well with Mally and carried him around by his short tail while slobbering all over the pup. Our animals were like family to us.

Our kids lived a carefree life among all the pets and animals on the farm. Whenever Michael was missing we knew he could be found at the staff houses sipping sweet, white tea with them while listening to the African beat from Rabesi's guitar. The monotonous, repetitive sounds had everybody mesmerized as they stared into the fire. My dad used to say that was the reason many black people had yellow eyes; too much staring into the fire with too much smoke.

Florah's five-year-old son, Lucky, showed him where to find inflated spherical plant balls in the bush. They really enjoyed the loud popping sounds when they squashed these flowers. The toys nature provided were much more interesting than shop toys.

"You know, Mom, Lucky is the luckiest boy alive. He doesn't have to go to school and can play in the bush all day long. He doesn't even have to bath every day! Why can't I live like that?" Michael had totally become a child of the African bush.

CHAPTER 24
MY DAD. MY MENTOR

On Tuesday morning 9 August 1994 my brother phoned me with very sad news. My dad had collapsed the previous day and things didn't look good.

We knew his health had been declining and that he was suffering from emphysema. Even when you think you have been preparing your heart for bad news, it still hits you hard.

I sat in front of my piano and played one of my dad's favourite songs, Be Still, my Soul. My dad had been a great shaper of my character and it was hard to imagine that he was dying. I was overcome by emotion and couldn't see the notes in front of me for all the tears steaming down my cheeks.

Gisèle wanted to know why I was crying. She said I mustn't forget that we have Jesus and that He will make me feel better if I let Him. Out of the mouth of babes!

We prepared to leave the following morning. Packing Clinton's suit for a funeral seemed utterly faithless. It felt like I had given up all hope for him to live, but I had to be sensible as well. It felt like I was condemning my dad to death by packing clothes for my family to wear to the funeral, while he was still alive.

Clinton drove the 2300 km in fourteen hours. On arrival I went straight to his bedside where I faced a person infinitely older than the person I had seen only three months before. One look into his eyes confirmed my worst fears. I knew that he would not be with us much longer. He knew and I knew. He was too weak to hug me, but smiled gently to show how glad he was to see us.

Alta had been keeping vigil at his bedside and I joined her. My dad was exhausted due to a lack of sleep. He was too short of breath to sleep for any length of time. Together we watched the sun rise. I had not slept in twenty-nine hours, but felt alert. I did not want to miss a single minute of the life he had left.

Just before lunch the following morning Dr Rudolf Laubscher confirmed that he was slipping away slowly. The NG Church minister came to his bedside and read Psalm 23 to him. The Lord is my Shepherd, I shall not want. I could see a mixture of peace and dread in his eyes. He loved the Lord and was ready to go, but the reality and proximity of death was still daunting.

He fell into a coma. We sat beside him as his breaths became shorter and further apart. He passed away later that afternoon without regaining consciousness. The grandfather clock in the entrance hall had stopped dead at the exact time of his death.

At the graveside I remembered his words of long ago. We must not think we are burying him, but only the shell that housed him for seventy-three years. He would be with the Lord in a much better place. We should be happy for him and not selfish by only thinking of our own grief. That was a tall order and I failed miserably.

CHAPTER 25
OSTRICH SMUGGLING

Our neighbours, ten kilometers from us, were accused of smuggling fertilized ostrich eggs from South Africa into Botswana. The Ostrich fraternity in South Africa was up in arms as it was a criminal offence to take live ostriches or fertile eggs out of South Africa.

This monopoly controlling the ostrich industry offered the Botswana government all assistance to catch trespassers. Ordinary permits for moving birds around inside Botswana had to be collected in the capitol, Gaborone, all of a sudden. Every ostrich in Botswana would have to be micro-chipped to track its movements.

We were ready to export to Spain, but our friends across the border were one jump ahead. A rumour that Botswana ostriches were rife with Newcastle's disease was spread in Europe. Soon the doors for export to Europe were closed, pending the outcome of an official enquiry that could easily take up to two years. The only sure outcome in our minds was that there would be many bankrupted ostrich farmers in Botswana. The Department of Wildlife had effectively destroyed a potentially booming farming sector in Botswana.

Many farmers had been smuggling. Because the indigenous bird looked quite different to its South African counterpart, farmers would have to explain the presence of South African birds on their farms. Clinton was the only ostrich farmer in Botswana who had legally imported South African stock many, many years ago. Now everyone wanted a letter from Clinton stating that he had sold them some South African birds, to save their backsides. Clinton had never resorted to bribing and was not going to start lying now. He was, however, so disgusted with the interference and immoral conduct of the South Africans that he was tempted to help his mates.

One day, when I am sure nobody will get into trouble, I might write a short story on the smuggling in Botswana. I know some chicks were brought through the Platjan Border Control Post in crates underneath other crates of chickens. Some baby ostriches were carried through the Limpopo River in boxes. Some grown birds were flown over in a small helicopter two at a time. One farmer chased a whole lot of adult birds over a low-water farm bridge and into a waiting truck on the Botswana side. The South Africans should rather have convinced Wildlife to control the number of legal imports of pre micro-chipped birds. They would then have had some sort of control.

I had learnt that the only point of arrival in this life is the moment you are born. The rest is a never-ending journey of discovering your strengths and weaknesses. There is no point at which you can feel that you have reached your destination of perfect contentment. There is always something else waiting to make you stronger.

The best you can do is live the present moment in the most positive way you are able to. There are always going to be challenges that seem too big for you. There are always going to be moments of pain and anguish. Your mindset is going to determine how you will cope.

I had committed my life to the Lord. That did not mean everything was going to be plain sailing, but it meant that whatever I was facing, I could be sure of the Lord's guidance and help. It was my choice to tackle a problem with courage and wisdom, or to decide that there was no way I was going to make it. My attitude will determine my altitude in every situation I have to face. The responsibility and privilege of choice remains my prerogative.

In South Africa the political tide was turning. The ANC had been un-banned and Nelson Mandela was freed after 27 years in prison. The country was set for its first ever truly democratic elections in May 1994.

We all knew the ANC would win, simply because 85% of South Africans had previously been denied the right to vote and they would all vote against the ruling Nationalist Party.

The future of South Africa was uncertain. Nobody could tell for sure that there would not be a bloodbath of unprecedented proportions. People in Botswana were asking what the South African whites were going to do. Would they take up arms and fight, or would they accept a black government?

My children had no idea what the fuss was about. They had grown up in a country where most of their friends were black. They were colour-blind and unaware of the racial tensions next door.

At this time Dr Quett Masire, the President of Botswana, came to visit us on the farm to see how Clinton was managing his ostriches. He had also started farming with these birds and was very interested to learn more about raising chicks, incubating eggs and the ostrich business in general.

Because of the political turmoil across the border, the Botswana Defense Force was called in to secure the area around our farm. Two Caspirrs were parked outside the entrance to the farm and the CID inspected every room in the house. A bathroom was dedicated to the exclusive use of the president. Mr John Motang was in charge of security in and around the house. There were so many soldiers and other VIP's around that Clinton decided to slaughter a couple of goats to provide everyone with something to eat.

The president was a vegetarian and I had prepared a spinach quiche for him. The rest of the party had to eat outside at the barbeque. The children were excited because of all the activity around the house. Michael just wanted to shoot with the soldiers' guns. Janine did cartwheels to impress the gang and Gisèle reprimanded her siblings to behave themselves. Sharon and Muller looked on in amusement.

Dr Masire is a kindly gentleman and took enough notice of the children to impress them. I took a video of them standing next to the president, looking very important and pleased with themselves. Michael was quiet and the president tickled him to force a little laugh from him. Michael had a habit of keeping his head quite still while rolling his eyes to the left and right to survey the scene. On the video this looks hilarious.

After all the polite conversation and a lovely meal, the men headed off to the ostriches.

The president shared our frustration concerning export permits, but refused to interfere as he respected the democratic process of his government departments. He is obviously a man of integrity, and as such, an exceptional leader an example to the rest of Africa.

The elections in South Africa surprised the whole world. Everything went off reasonable smoothly and the world didn't end when the first black government came into power. A government of National Unity, with the ANC working together with the Nationalist Party, ruled the new Rainbow Nation. There were many teething problems and doom prophets, but overall people were reasonable optimistic. Nelson Mandela emerged as a leader who gained the respect of the world. He could so easily have acted out of revenge, but he chose the way of forgiveness. He set the example and most of his cabinet followed.

There was one serious concern for landowners in South Africa, though. The ANC wanted previously disadvantaged citizens to own more land in the RSA. The policy of Land Reform was too advanced for the people who had not learnt enough about the basics of business. Huge, fertile farms were bought by the government and handed over to these people, only to fall to pieces after a short time. Whites were quick to point out that Blacks were simply not able to farm productively and that they were unable to build up anything, but very good at destroying everything. The Blacks blamed everything that went wrong on the apartheid system, and the Whites blamed it all on the incompetent Blacks.

A couple of weeks later Janine fell from the old Scotia tree and broke her arm late one afternoon The border post closed at 4pm and we had to get her to a hospital, the closest one being in Pietersburg in South Africa. We took a chance and were allowed through. The doctor set the arm, but decided to call in a surgeon to see why there was no pulse in her wrist. After a further two and a half hours all the severed arteries had been joined again, but we were told that it could take up to five years for her to regain her small motor movements in her hand. The nerves had been damaged badly. We prayed for a speedy healing and trusted God to work a miracle. After six months Janine was able to colour, paint and write as well as before her fall. We stood in awe of our great God and healer.

Faith in Him never fails.

CHAPTER 26
THE LAND OF CANAAN

After much effort and frustration, we were given a permit to export adult birds to Andorra. An hotelier from Pretoria who had been involved in our business for some time, organized for them to fly out from Gaborone International Airport. He also promised to refund the enormous amounts of money I had pumped into the farm from the proceeds of the sale of my shop, Petals and Pleats. The birds landed safely in Europe, but we never smelled a cent. He said that the price of the birds had fallen so much that the cost of the flight could not even be covered by the money he got for the ostriches.

We had had enough of empty promises and lies. We were fed up and pretty broke. We would have to make other plans to survive.

Clinton had to go to Louis Trichardt, a town in South Africa, to have a cylinder head skimmed. While he was waiting he went for lunch at the Spur. There he met Carel, an estate agent, who took him to see a farm in the Levubu district 50 km away. Clinton told him that he had no money to invest in property and that there was no way he could buy a farm. Carel took him anyway.

What he saw there blew him over. A sub-tropical valley where bananas, nuts, avocado's and various other fruit were grown unfolded in front of his eyes. A mere fifty kilometers away the landscape was completely different; the bushveld of the Northern Province.

The soil was deep and fertile. An average of one and a half meters of rain per annum is normal in this most wind free area in the country. Compared to the dry landscape of Botswana, this was the Garden of Eden.

Clinton came back and I could see he was very impressed with what he had seen. At the same time he was depressed about our lack of finances to do anything about it.

I wanted to go back to the Cape, but agreed to have a look at this property in Levubu. I prayed for guidance from the Lord. I knew that I would have to listen carefully and not allow my emotions to dictate to me. That was going to be hard, considering all that had happened in the past nine years to us financially.

After I had seen the farm in Levubu, I shared Clinton's enthusiasm. Here I could garden to my heart's content. As far as the eye could see, rolling hills of green fruit trees, bananas and other sub-tropical plants unfolded like the pages of a story book.

We faxed through the feasibility study to my brother. He flew up to inspect the farm. Two days later we signed the deed of sale. We managed to get a full loan from the bank to purchase the farm, with my brother standing guarantee for a third of the amount. The farm, however, was to service the full bond.

We formed El Shaddai Trust with Andries' and our children as the beneficiaries. El Shaddai is the Hebrew name for God meaning He who is more than enough. There seemed to be more than enough food around here, at least. After nine years in a semi-desert, this was the land of milk and honey, or rather fruit and nuts.

We left Botswana with mixed feelings. We had had the most interesting life, even if we never really made money from our farming enterprises. Our children were growing up and would need to attend good schools. Home schooling had been to their advantage academically, but we wanted them to experience the social education of team sport and school life.

Levubu borders on the old Venda homeland. After the ANC took over, all homelands were incorporated back into the Republic of South Africa. The famous Kruger National Park's Northern gate, Punda Maria, is about sixty kilometers from Levubu. This fertile valley was also known to be the pantry of the Northern Province.

The majority of Whites in this area have always been far right wing supporters. We found it difficult to explain to our children when they heard racial remarks at school.

Politically we pined for Botswana. In South Africa patience and mutual understanding were in short supply. We could understand Setswana, but had no clue about Venda, which made communication with our workers difficult. The foreman, Thomas Chauke, could understand Afrikaans and handled all staff matters.

We had been invited for a barbeque at the Maritz's farm. Lisa Maritz was one of the first friends Gisèle had made at Levubu Primary School. Her parents were kind enough to extend a hand of friendship to us. We went in the pick-up with the kids on the back. As we passed the filling station near our entrance gate, we heard shots ringing out. Clinton shouted for the kids to fall down flat and he sped away. We had just witnessed an armed robbery on our doorstep. We called the police and told them what had happened. We could also tell them that the getaway car was a white Citi Golf. The following day the police came to tell us that the owner of Dzananwa Filling Station had been shot dead during the robbery. My word! We were shocked. Had our South Africa become so lawless and dangerous! Had we put our heads in a bees' nest by moving back? We were very pleased that Tao was our guard dog and that nobody had ever dared to casually wander into our security-fenced yard. Clinton immediately got us two more Boer Bulls to guard our home.

Work on Laatsgevonden, the name of the farm, seemed never-ending. Bananas were harvested throughout the year. Fertilizing, irrigating, harvesting, weeding, packaging and transporting of the fruit and nuts were everyday chores. Clinton worked very hard, but enjoyed every minute.

Michael, who had been driving since the age of six, jumped at every opportunity to drive around the farm in the Land Rover. He was sent to fetch and carry boxes, people and whatever else that needed to be transported on the farm.

At school the children made new friends and really enjoyed the afternoon sport. Gisèle was now in grade five, the smallest in her class, but as strong as an ox and excelled at swimming and gymnastics. Academically she was very strong as well.

Michael has very large feet and there was nobody who could swim faster than him. Clinton's swimming coaching at Peg's Valley was paying dividends. In fact, everything he taught our children on the sports field, they applied diligently. On the athletics track he proved to be a good sprinter, hurdler and high jumper.

Janine was five when she started gymnastics at a club in Louis Trichardt. Her natural ability and the good coaching at the club earned her provincial colours after a year and a half.

I used to do my grocery shopping in Louis Trichardt while the kids did gymnastics. I often sat and watched them practice until one day when I got on the beam to see if I could still do a balance stand. Giel Nel, the boys' coach saw me and asked me to start training with the veteran team (the over twenty-fives). I laughed at his suggestion. Imagine a forty-two-year old in a leotard! But Clinton encouraged me and I started training. Seven months later my body had undergone a metamorphosis and I felt fit and good. I made the Northern Province team and competed at the Senior South African Championships. It felt weird to have my family watching me instead of the other way around. I managed to end as the silver medallist and my hubby was so proud of his wife. My kids were chuffed too, although they did remind me that the level at which I competed and my opposition were not too hot. It was great fun and encouraged me to believe I wasn't quite over the wall yet.

An older boy, much bigger than Michael, picked a fight with him during the lunch-break at school one day. Gisèle saw him sitting on top of Michael and rushed in to save her little brother. She ran, jumped and landed with her knees on the bully's back, almost breaking his ribs. The fight was over instantly. Blood is thicker than water, Michael discovered, and nobody looked for trouble with Gisèle again.

Gisèle had become quite a looker and the boys tried to gain her favour all the time. There was one boy who caught her attention. His parents farmed with mangoes on the other side of town. Albertus came to visit her one Saturday afternoon, accompanied by his friend, Divan. Lisa Maritz, Gisèle's best friend, was visiting too and the foursome walked down to the dam. A very old, very big crocodile had been living in this dam for as long as people could remember. Albertus waded into the water to pick a water lily for the object of his affection. The others tried to stop him by warning him of the crocodile in the dam, but he picked the flower and swam out quickly before disaster could strike. He presented her with this gift and received a kiss on the cheek as thanks. This was quite heroic for a boy of eleven and the girls thought he was very brave. Divan thought he was mad.

I was called in by the headmaster, Nico Botes, one morning. My first thought was that Michael had been naughty again. Nico closed the door of the office. I sat down and waited. The next moment he started laughing and I wasn't sure what was happening. Apparently Gisèle had punched Divan on the eye in class. He had ignored her pleas to stop throwing around her pencil case, so she decided to sort him out with the fist! Nico explained that, according to school rules, he was forced to call me in, but the staff all agreed that she had done them a great service. Divan could be rather difficult and this lesson would be beneficial to him in his social education.

Michael's big mate, Leo van der Walt, often came to visit. Leo didn't have upper front teeth. He said he had contracted chicken pox on his gums and that had caused his permanent teeth to go into hiding. His cute little face was framed by protruding ears.

Leo and Michael decided to camp next to the crocodile dam one evening. I thought this idea a little adventurous for two nine year olds, but Clinton said not to worry. He doubted whether their bravery was going to last the night. They left in the pick-up, pitched a tent fifty yards away in the macadamia land and had Mally to guard them. At midnight I heard a vehicle coming into the yard slowly. I looked out of the window and saw the two of them in the pick-up. After twenty minutes they had not come into the house and I went outside to see what was happening. The windows were completely fogged up and the two were sleeping soundly with Mally sitting on Leo's lap. I tapped against the window. They woke up with a start. Of course they were not afraid! They had just come home to fetch coffee. I couldn't recall either ever having enjoyed coffee before. I told them to come inside and get to bed. Absolutely not. They were having a great time in their tent and wanted to go back. I asked them to open a window slightly so that Mally could breathe and then I went back to bed. The two of them slept in the pick-up in the yard all night. Early the following morning they went back to collect their tent and no word was spoken about their whereabouts that evening.

Our neighbours, Johan and Gilly Boshof, had an aviary with beautiful birds. Johan hand-reared three cockatiels for the children and brought them over when they were big enough to feed themselves. Each child had a cage ready in their room for their new pets. I allowed them these pets on the condition that they clean out the cages regularly and care for their birds themselves.

These cockatiels were so tame that they sat on the children's shoulders in the mornings at the breakfast table, pecking away at their cereal. Sometimes they would peck at the kids' mouths in the hope of sharing their half chewed food. Janine's bird was called Birdie and danced beautifully when one whistled to it. Birdie could say its name and repeat tunes like "Jan Pierewiet".

True to life, pets bring so much joy and also such heartache when something happens to them. One morning Michael took his cockatiel out of its cage without realizing his window was still open. It flew out never to be found again. He was heartbroken. I told him to think about it this way. May be it was enjoying its freedom so much that it simply wanted to stay outside with all the other wild birds. He wasn't really convinced, but would rather believe this than think it was caught by a hawk or some other bird of prey.

Gisèle thought Birdie was a silly name for a bird, until we had to look after her friend's hamster one weekend. She wasn't too keen to take care of the hamster and really lost it when I told her that the hamster's name was also Birdie. I was only joking, but canned myself at her reaction. The fact that she had believed me, explained her perception of the hamster's owner.

Typical of siblings, arguing was as common as breakfast in our household. The never-ending bickering about who got to sit in front in the car on the way to school forced me to lay down rules.

We rotated this privilege on a weekly basis. That worked well, but they quickly found other topics to dispute. I decided that we would pray all the way to school. Each child would be given the opportunity to say a short prayer. That would keep them positively occupied for eight minutes each morning as well as lower my levels of frustration. For the first three kilometers we shared the main road with many taxis that had no intention of obeying traffic laws. A taxi driver would often stop in the middle of this busy road and cause a traffic jam of note. I was a bad example to my children when this happened. Invariable I would call them terrible names, only to confess my sin a minute later when we had turned off on the quiet road to town. I always started my prayer with a supplication to God to forgive me for the language I had just used. One day, in the middle of my prayer, Janine told me to stop praying. I was rather taken aback at this interruption and asked her what she meant.

"Mommy, you can't ask for forgiveness if you are not sorry!"

"But of course I am sorry."

"No, you are not!" she insisted

"How can you say that?" I defended myself.

"If you were really sorry, you would not do it every morning."

I was amazed at the insight and wisdom coming from my six year old. What she had said was absolutely true and kept me thinking all day. I vowed to try harder to control myself. Indeed, remorse was a fleeting emotion. The problem was not the poor driving from the taxis, but my lack of patience and wisdom in the situation. I had been fooling myself all along, thinking my slate was clean after a short prayer of forgiveness. I needed to turn away from this sinful habit. That alone would prove I was genuinely sorry.

Gisèle's prayer one morning tried our self-control to its limits. She had had an argument with Michael about his table manners at breakfast and was obviously still angry with him. She asked the Lord to help him to chew softer and eat nicely. Michael's eyes shot open and he was just about to launch his verbal attack when she continued, "But thank you Lord for the other nice things he does for us." He was speechless and we all burst out laughing followed by quick apologies in case the Lord was offended. I assured them Jesus was also laughing, but might view the prayer as slightly manipulative on Gisèle's part.

I did not want my children to become religious. I wanted them to have a real relationship of respect, love and fun with Jesus. Children are very quick to sense insincerity. A relationship with the Lord means little if you can't be honest and sincere with Him. I am sure He has to have a good sense of humour to forgive us all our masquerades.

The annual Fruit Festival in Levubu was the highlight of the year. This event was organized by the primary school and considered the main fund raising project for the year. Apart from all the fruit stalls, there were all kinds of games and activities to entertain old and young. The go-carts were very popular, in spite of the dirt track winding around some huge trees. Witte Beetge and I decided to dice each other. After three rounds we were banned from the track for reckless driving. Witte just shook his head and told Clinton his wife had turned into a raving lunatic in the go-cart. My children could not believe that their mother, who was always admonishing their dad to drive carefully, could possibly be guilty as charged. Michael assured them that Witte's remark was justified. He had witnessed his mother antics on the track and was not at all surprised that she was banned. I don't know what had come over me, but it felt really good to throw caution to the wind and break every rule I had made concerning road safety. There was a side to me I had just started discovering.

"That's my girl!" Clinton gave me a hug, but muttered softly, "Blooming crazy woman. I'll sort you out later. Hope you're now going to cut me some slack in the car for a while!"

I liked things to be organized and neat. After so many years of dirt and dust, struggling and persevering, I needed structure and order around me. Whenever I spent enough time with the Lord, I became calm, focused and the eternal optimist. Then the outcome would always be good. Whenever I zoomed in on the pressure of the moment, I turned into a control freak. No, that is a little harsh. May be just a little bit of a control freak. The point is: I thought my way was the only right way. I had been given a new heart of faith by the Lord, but still had the old rotten head on top of it. The process of renewing the mind is a slow process that requires a daily feed on the Word of God. Old thought patterns have to change. Faith comes by hearing and digesting the truth found in the Bible, and then doing it. This requires discipline and trusting God - not very easy when you look at the size of the problem instead of at God's ability to solve it.

We had a big scare one Sunday morning on the farm. André and Pat Campbell and their son Lawrence were visiting us. Clinton and André took the children with them when they went looking for a wounded bushbuck. The children were all sitting on the back of the pick-up when one wheel got stuck in a hole. Clinton accelerated in an attempt to get the wheel free. They did not realize that the "hole" was actually an underground bees' nest. The spinning wheel caused the disturbed bees to fly out and attack en masse. Before they could get away, the bees had stung them all and continued their attack relentlessly. They fled away from the stuck vehicle, but the bees followed them and continued their revenge.

Back home Pat and I had prepared tea and carrot cake and were waiting for them to join us on the patio. I heard someone crying out for me and saw Michael outside the fence running towards the gate. I knew something must be wrong. Where were the others and why did he not have a shirt on? I ran towards him and saw hundreds of stings all over his face, chest and back. I was shocked and tried to think of the correct treatment for bee sting.

He told me to get to Clinton and the others quickly as they had been stung badly. I quickly gave Pat some vinegar (I had read somewhere that vinegar dabbed on to the skin helps) and asked her to scrape off the stings with a blunt knife while I drove to find the others.

I saw Clinton and the children walking very slowly and unsteadily in the road. They looked drugged. My pulse was racing as I realized the danger they were in. They got into the car silently and we went looking for André. We found him lying under a banana tree. He breathed with difficulty and we got him into the car as quickly as possible.

Back home I phoned the hospital and asked for a doctor to be ready for us. The closest hospital was in Louis Trichardt fifty kilometers away. Gisèle started vomiting before we left and I was worried. They had all been stung by hundreds of bees and I knew they would be in trouble soon. Pat and I drove in two cars and we chased like madmen to get to the hospital. En route everyone in the car remained silent. The only noise came from the children on the back seat vomiting in the little rubbish bin I gave them. Whenever I thought they were too quiet, I would call out their names one by one to check if they were still conscious. All sound they could muster was a feeble "uhh". I prayed non-stop and pleaded with the Lord to keep them alive and to help me to drive safely and quickly. At the first stop street I thought Pat was going to crash into the back of our car. She didn't know the road well and was frantically chasing to keep up with me.

At the hospital the doctor was waiting. André was injected in the heart, Clinton in the stomach and they were all put on drips and given pills under their tongues. The entire emergency room was in chaos as the doctor ran around trying to monitor everyone. The nurses started scraping out the stings and counted more than four hundred on Michael alone. He had been stung inside his ears, his nose, his lips and his entire upper body. Janine, who, according to André, had so many bees on her that he could not make out which was her front or back, seem to be the most stable of the lot. True to her nature, she had stood still and did not slap at the bees, so she was not stung too badly. The nurse took out just more than a hundred stings on her head alone.

After six hours under his watchful eye, the doctor said we could take them home. He could not believe that they had recovered so quickly and declared them very lucky to be alive at all. We knew luck had nothing to do with it. That evening they slept well, but they looked terrible the following day. Their faces were swollen and their eyes were slits. They resembled badly beaten up gangsters. There was not too much wrong with their sense of humour, though, as they started teasing one another about who looked the worst. Clinton gathered us all to give special thanks to God who had saved their lives.

Ever since this incident, my children are very wary of bees. The doctor said that they could become allergic to bee venom after this, but, praise the Lord, they have not had any allergic reaction, in spite of the odd sting they suffered occasionally in the years that followed.

I don't know how I would have coped with this emergency if I did not have Jesus in whom to trust. He had come through for us time and time again and the gratitude I felt towards my Saviour grew steadily in my heart.

All our fruit and vegetables were taken to the markets in Johannesburg and Pretoria by Landman Transport. Johan and Francis Landman have identical twins, Sariana and Jolandi. We became good friends and were often invited to spend a weekend on their farm in the Bushveld. On one such occasion, it happened to be mopani worm season. These caterpillars were cooked in salt water, dried out in the sun and then sold for good money to the locals by their staff that lived on the farm. Mopani worms are considered a delicacy by most Africans and of course, as gross as they may look, are a very good source of protein. Gisèle quite liked eating them. She said they tasted like dried sausage.

We were watching the women squeezing out the insides and breaking off the heads in one quick movement before dropping them into a drum of boiling water. Gisèle took a big, fat, live worm and dangled it above her open mouth, pretending to want to eat it. We shrieked in horror. Jolandi could not believe this and Gisèle, having had her moment of fun, dropped it back into the bag with thousands of other worms awaiting the pot.

During game drives on Johan's farm, we saw giraffe and many different kinds of buck. He was slowly stocking up on more game. This beautiful place was an idyllic escape for a weekend after the long hours of work during the week. The children and I painted a tablecloth and drew all the funny incidents of the weekend like a story on the cloth. There was Johan, carrying a jerry can of fuel on his exhausted shoulder when we ran out of diesel during a game drive, Janine with blood on her forehead after a disasterous back flip into the pool, Michael, Jolandi, Sariana and Gisèle as the characters they played in the concert they had put on for the adults one evening, and Clinton sitting back relaxing with a brandy and coke in his hand.

While watching the sunset in the quiet dusk one evening, Clinton had us in hysterics with a true story about game poaching in the Kruger National Park. Sakkie, an absolute character in Levubu, and some mates had invited the new headmaster on a hunt. This chap was an extremely law-abiding citizen and should have smelled a rat when he heard the hunt would be at night. En route he asked where they would be hunting.

"On my grandfather Paul's farm," Sakkie replied innocently.

As they approached the park, they veered off to the left and entered through a small private, obviously illegal gate. After they had shot some buck with a spotlight and silencers they started on their return journey. At this stage the headmaster knew they could end up in jail and was frantic. To make matters worse, on the main road back, they saw a police roadblock ahead with all the lights flashing. Abruptly they stopped. Sakkie stripped naked, got onto the back of the truck where he stood on top of the buck, tied a rope around his own neck and to the railings of the pick-up and told his mate to drive straight towards he roadblock. The poor headmaster needed clean underwear at this point and begged them to drop him off next to the side of the road. They ignored his pleas and drove on. The police waved them down and they stopped. Sakkie, at this stage, had begun snarling and spitting on the back and started swaying around like a demented person. The superstitious policeman took one look at this creature and decided he wasn't going to get involved with a mad white man in the dark. Without so much as a look to inspect their load, he stood back and told them to get away fast. They didn't need a second invitation and sped off home. Needless to say, the headmaster never went hunting in Levubu again without being accompanied by the reverend.

Every place has its characters and we tend to remember these people better than others who were perhaps wealthier or more powerful. Laughter is like good medicine to the soul and we found plenty to laugh about and enough to be concerned about. Clinton had this amazing ability to bring hope and joy into every potentially stressful situation. His plans never dried up, neither did his determination to succeed. If something didn't work out the way we had planned, he would be ready to try something else. I never saw him fall into any state of depression.

The farm was doing well and our produce was in great demand. Market agents from all over the country phoned after seeing the quality of our bananas and sweet potatoes, but our bond repayments were huge and we could not waste a cent, despite the good turnover.

At Petals and Pleats I had a small turnover with huge profits. To this day the turnover of a business does not impress me. I am only interested in the net profit it produces. Sometimes a big turnover can cause a big ego with big problems and little profit. I think the trick is not to become too big too quickly.

The new land redistribution policy was causing major concern in the Levubu agricultural circles. Many farms had land claims registered against them. That basically means that certain ethnic groups claimed that the land had belonged to their ancestors and that they had the right to claim it back. When we bought Laatsgevonden, we were assured that there were no claims registered against the farm. This turned out to be disputable in the eyes of the government when they further extended the deadline for the lodging of land claims. The white farmers felt that many of these claims were illegal and founded on claims that could not be proved. The situation became a deadlock. The government didn't know how to handle these issues and their indecision caused the banks to withhold further credit to farmers in possession of land under dispute.

Nobody would invest in land that could be repossessed. Eventually the price of this fertile ground started falling and more and more farmers found that their equity, in terms of ground owned, had lost value fast. Here I think of the Israelite scouts who came back to report on the land of Canaan. Ten of them said that the people living in Canaan were giants and "We looked like grasshoppers in OUR eyes". At this stage most people felt like grasshoppers fighting off the giants. We needed a Joshua and Caleb to tell us that we could conquer the giants of inefficient government departments.

There were talks of the government repossessing most of the farms in Levubu and returning the land to ethnic groups who had laid claims to it. After farming here for nearly four years, we tried to sell the farm, but no individual was going to take that chance. A group of Venda buyers tried to get the government to help them to buy the farm, and all sorts of promises were made, but nothing materialized. We could not help wondering if South Africa was going the same way as Zimbabwe.

The bank called up the loan and we were in dire straits financially. We had been in financial difficulties so often that we did what always worked. We prayed and trusted in God for strategy. We knew, no matter what we could lose materially, we could never lose Him or His love and provision. He had looked after us thus far, so we would praise and serve Him in good times and bad times.

Our church in Levubu had been so great. We were surrounded by people who prayed with us and for us. I was privileged to be part of the worship team at the Family Church where I played the keyboard in the team. At home, while practicing the songs for the following Sunday, I poured out my heart to the Lord in songs I composed as I played. They couldn't have been too bad as the dogs all came closer and lay at my feet under the piano. May be they were lulled to sleep by my slow melancholy melodies. Whatever the case, I enjoyed my time with the Lord and found that His peace guarded my heart against fear. His love drives out all fear, I kept telling myself.

Our neighbour, Piet van Wyk, bought the bottom half of the farm bordering his. The top section of the farm was eventually bought by the government and Braam van Wyk, Piet's nephew, managed it for a syndicate of Vendas.

CHAPTER 27
THE RETURN OF THE NATIVE

We moved down to the Cape to my mother's house in Bredasdorp. This was to be a short-term arrangement as we were hoping to settle in the district.

The children were booked into school in Bredasdorp. Michael and Janine were in grades four and six respectively and Gisèle was in grade nine at the high school. Gisèle had started school at age five under the British School system in Botswana. At Levubu Junior School Janine was not allowed to start school before she had turned six and Michael, having always been taught through the medium of English, was put in a class of children his own age. He was a year younger than all the other children in his grade and the headmaster advised us to put him with the correct age group for the sake of his rugby as well as the fact that he would now have to change to Afrikaans medium. Initially I was opposed to this idea, as he was very strong academically, but then decided it would be beneficial to him in the long run. He had never spelled or read in Afrikaans before.

I had attended Bredasdorp Junior School as a child and was very impressed with the standard of education there. The headmaster,

Johan Burger, welcomed the children warmly and they made new friends quickly. I couldn't help feeling guilty about uprooting my children so often. I was hoping we hadn't scarred them emotionally by all our moving around. Michael had once asked me, while I was home-schooling them at Peg's Valley, if we were nomadic. He had just learned about nomadic tribes in Africa and thought we fitted the definition well.

I once had an in depth conversation with the three of them and asked them to tell me honestly how all of this had affected them. While admitting they were missing their old friends, they also pointed out to me that very few kids had so many friends across the country. Gisèle was still corresponding with junior school friends from Botswana, now living in the UK. I could see the strength of their relationship with Jesus in the way they handled everything that was dished out to them and I was eternally grateful for His presence in their lives.

All three attended swimming coaching sessions with a professional coach. This often meant getting up at five in the mornings. The training was hard, but paid good dividends. Gisèle was awarded full colours for making the Boland swimming team. Michael and Janine both swam for South Boland. All three became the top swimmers of their schools.

On the athletics track Michael excelled as a hurdler. In his grade seven year he received the prize for the best track athlete at school. Janine and Michael were both included in the Boland Gymnastics tumbling team. Academically all three were doing brilliantly and we were so proud of them. Our children were examples to us of how to make the best of every situation.

During our stay with my mom, she was incredibly loving and caring. She told me a story about Michael and two of his friends that made me laugh. She had been to the grocery shop and on her way home she spotted him, Albert Potgieter and two other friends walking past the post office, closely following a couple of girls ahead of them. When the girls went into the post office, they pretended to be engaged in a serious conversation with the petrol attendant, but as soon as these ladies, only too aware of the boys behind them, strolled out and down the street, they followed as casually as they could while obviously grading the talent ahead of them.

My babies were growing up fast and Clinton watched his girls closely. He warned them that all boys had the same thing on their minds - that meant not to be trusted around his daughters. I had to smile at that one, coming from him.

Alta was getting married to Louis Kruger, and we had another happy event to look forward to. Her wedding was held at a lovely venue out in the Bredasdorp district. Marina du Toit had this beautiful restaurant on their farm, called Antoinette's, and she made sure the food and décor were perfect. It was a small wedding with only the immediate family in attendance, and we all enjoyed this intimate celebration tremendously. Alta has always been very close to us and we were happy that she had found someone to share her life with. In his speech Clinton reminded Louis that he would be watched closely by all of us. We are all very protective of Alta.

Gisèle and Janine

We had brought down a truckload of plants from our nursery in Levubu. Kobus and I started selling them to nurseries in Cape Town. Soon I started landscaping again. Parklands, a new development close to the sea near Bloubergstrand, was the first area we worked. Alta lived very close to this area in Table View and we stayed with her while we landscaped gardens there. Gigi gave someone in Constantia our contact number and we landed our first big job in the Southern Suburbs. We needed Clinton's expertise with the irrigation system and he joined our little business. There was so much opportunity in this line that we were kept very busy. The only drawback was the traffic we had to negotiate every day. We worked as far as Kommetjie with our team of farm workers we had brought from Bredasdorp. The city was a new experience for them and a little overwhelming I think.

We were doing all right and could make ends meet, but the never ending rat race and traffic jams from morning to night eventually got to us all after two and a half years.

Clinton was never someone for the city life. He was such an experienced irrigation expert that his knowledge could be applied more profitably in the agricultural arena. Our hopes of buying land in the Bredasdorp district, which was an extensively dry-land farming community, did not seem like a good idea any longer.

Clinton had attended Grey High School in Port Elizabeth and Michael was very keen to follow in his father's footsteps. He had listened to so many of Clinton's school stories that he was absolutely set on going to Grey. During the June holidays in his grade six year at primary school, we took him to see the school. He had been accepted and was so excited. The grounds and buildings are magnificent and impressed us immensely. We stayed over in the Senior School hostel with Anton and Ingrid Scholtz. Anton has been senior housemaster at Grey for many years. His father, Piet Scholtz had been our doctor in Cradock and had also been my doctor when Gisèle was born. Clinton and Anton had known each other since childhood.

We met the Junior School headmaster, Mr. Pearson, and he wanted Michael to complete his last year of junior school at Grey Junior the following year. In the end we decided to rather send him at the start of his high school career. He was doing so well at Bredasdorp Primary School and our finances would be spared a little for another year. Port Elizabeth is a good 650 km from Bredasdorp.

Michael was sent to boarding school in 2001 at the age of 13. He looked so smart in his new school uniform when we dropped him off. He was so proud and excited about his dad's old school. He saw his dad's name on the big honours board in the school hall. When Clinton showed him the bench in the foyer where he often had to wait for a hiding from the headmaster I thought Michael's laugh sounded a little nervous. In the prefects study at the boarding house Clinton showed him where he had enjoyed the camaraderie of his old school mates. Michael's friend from Cape Town, Matthew Lake, Tanky Lake's son, was the only boy he knew when he started at Grey. Tanky had also attended Grey many moons before. When we left we were asked not to contact him for three weeks. This was to help him settle down and bond with all the other new boys in the same boat. They would have to help each other and not run to mom or dad when the going got tough.

On our way back to Bredasdorp we had long moments of silence. Clinton knew from experience that the first term at boarding school would be a period of adapting to strict codes of conduct, and that life could be hard at times. He had received his first hiding on his first night as a border for hitting a prefect. Clinton went to Grey Junior in grade seven and was not used to prefects being the same age as him. When this boy, who was also in grade seven, told him he was not allowed sweets in his dormitory, he did not believe that he was a prefect and told him to get lost. This boy demanded that he hand over his chocolate. When Clinton refused, the prefect grabbed him by his pajama top. The next moment the prefect was man down after Clinton hit him with his fist. This incident was reported to the housemaster who gave Clinton a couple of lashes with the cane. Furious, he went back to his dormitory and beat the prefect again for not fighting his own battles. Another hiding followed and Clinton learnt to respect authority, no matter in which size or shape it came. I quietly prayed that Michael would be obedient and walk the line.

Gisèle and Janine were convinced Michael was going to be turned into a perfect gentleman in record time. Clinton laughed and said that part comes from the way you have been raised and the example your parents set. The school could only build on the foundations already laid in your home.

Midway through the first term we went to fetch Michael for the weekend. We had missed his happy laughter and boyish pranks so much. When the girls saw him they burst out laughing. He had a very pronounced side parting in his hair —not cool at all! All the new pots had this hairstyle and they looked very different to the older boys with neat but modern hairstyles. Instead of the perfect gentleman they had expected, an angry little boy put his suitcase in the boot and asked his dad to drive off. He had had enough of being shunted around and just wanted to relax with his family. After a while his mood lifted and we laughed together at all the crazy things the new pots had to do. He was very happy at school and especially loved the sport, but had to get used to being shunted around by the seniors. He disliked unfairness intensely, and soon learned that this was part of life and that he would have to come to terms with it quickly.

After a visit to the Karoo where he had grown up, Clinton realized that of all the places he had been, the Karoo and its special people were still closest to his heart. He knew everybody. I could sense what was coming and braced myself. How could we do this to our children again? I didn't even want to count the number of schools Gisèle had attended. She had one and a half years of school left. She had established herself as a leader at every level and was highly regarded by her teachers at Bredasdorp High School. She was an excellent student and sportswoman, very involved in cultural activities, editor of the school newspaper and very popular among the scholars. Michael was no problem as he had already started school at Grey. Janine was young, happy and completely content as long as we were together. She had two very close friends in Bredasdorp, Retha and Teena, and she was going to miss them tremendously.

We went to Somerset East for the weekend and had a wonderful time looking around and getting a feel for the place. Sandra and John Vie had gracefully offered us the use of their home for the weekend. Clinton had decided that, if we should ever move back to the Karoo, this would be the town in which we would settle.

Somerset East is a very old town, small and beautifully kept. It lies at the foot of the Boschberg Mountains and falls within the long, narrow stretch of land called the Smaldeel. This area receives more rain than the surrounding Karoo landscape and has a more moderate climate too. Port Elizabeth is situated 180 km to the south of Somerset East.

The most appealing characteristic of the Karoo is the brutal honesty of the land and its people. This is a dry part of South Africa, not deceptively inviting to the senses and downright ugly in some parts. The beautiful areas are often off the beaten track and come as a complete surprise and delight. The people of this land are hardy and tough, but basically generous and kind. I could do honesty and hardship any day, but yearned for a place we could call home. I was ready for anything as long as it meant settling down. We had been the proverbial nomads for long enough.

We had been transplanted regularly and could never put down deep roots anywhere. In a way this helped us to nurture only one deep root of faith - in our Lord and Saviour, Jesus Christ alone. He became our only source of hope, the only well that never dried up, the only stable foundation on which to build a future.

Clinton was offered a job, marketing wool for a company owned by a consortium of farmers. Andrew van Lingen was a director on the board and this alone inspired confidence in the company. Andrew is Carl's cousin. They had been bred from the same stock of generations of integrity. This offer turned our minds to the very real possibility of returning to our heartland.

On our way back to Bredasdorp, the girls and I had a heart-to-heart conversation about our proposed future in Somerset East. I needed them to be very frank with me. I wanted them to tell me we were crazy, I felt they had the right to accuse us of being the most irresponsible parents in the world. God knows I felt we had failed them in providing stability in terms of a permanent address. Guilt, another useless and destructive emotion, gripped me and demanded its pound of flesh.

I was humbled by their response.

"Mom, we have never felt insecure. We know you and Dad have always done the best you could. Your love and devotion to each other and to us have been more than most other children have ever had. We are happy wherever we are, as long as we are together. Let's do this!"

The world and all its troubles seem to lift from my shoulders. Their blessing was of paramount importance to me.

"Lord, what have we done to deserve these children?" I asked silently.

"Nothing. They are My grace in action," He replied gently.

CHAPTER 28
THE FULL CIRCLE

We looked at a couple of houses in Somerset, knowing we had limited funds. I had invested some of the money I inherited from my dad in property in Cape Town where my sister now lived. She was quitting teaching and would be able to buy me out. We could use this money as a deposit on a house.

Clinton met Gerhard du Preez, a lawyer in Somerset East, and he showed us a property for sale next to his home. This four-bedroom house is called Castlemaine and is built on a very large piece of ground, in fact, on three large plots. There is a big swimming pool, a small reservoir cleverly converted into a barbeque area and an enormous landscaped garden. The formal lounge is the size of a small house. The beautiful oregan floors gleamed warmly in the afternoon sun. All the rooms are spacious and sunny. We all fell in love with this place the moment we laid eyes on it.

This property was too expensive for us, but Dupie said we should put in an offer anyway. Clinton agreed and gave Dupie a figure on which to work. We were so excited, but also realized that it was a long shot.

We had learnt to trust God for the impossible. Whenever you are able to do something in your own strength, you don't need faith to accomplish it, but when it is too big for you, you have to put your faith in the Lord. God is pleased when we show faith in Him. He has shown us on numerous occasions that nothing is impossible for Him.

Alta declared faithfully that the Lord would help us to get this house. She just felt confirmation in her spirit and believed it would come to pass. Clinton was on his way to Bedford a week later when he got the call from Dupie. The offer had been accepted. He made a u-turn, rushed back to Somerset and signed the documents before anybody could change their minds.

We were absolutely thrilled and blown away. The children immediately staked their claims on the bedrooms. We had taken photo's of the place when we viewed it and now spent a lot of time looking at each picture, deciding what piece of furniture should go where.

At the beginning of the June holidays we left Bredasdorp and moved to Somerset East. Gisèle enrolled herself at Gill College. She had decided to start at this prestigious old school immediately, instead of waiting for the new school year. Clinton and I went to see the headmaster of Gill Junior School, Deon Bekker, who warmly welcomed us and Janine was set to start on the first day of the new term.

We had to wait until the end of June to move in. The tenants had a lease until then. Jac and Idelette Troskie kindly offered her mother's home to us for the two weeks we had to wait. I started watering and reviving the garden immediately. My children and I worked like Trojans in the garden, pruning the roses, cutting away dead wood from the trees and basically clearing out overgrown sections of the garden. Michael, in his enthusiasm to clear away dry palm branches, got a long palm thorn stuck in his hand. We ended up in Dr Tobie Louw's surgery where he had to cut it out and stitch the hand.

Once we had moved into our lovely home and settled down, we started socializing with our neighbours. Fort Street, Sally van Niekerk declared, was THE STREET in town. It was also the only street that held an annual street barbeque. Sally and Thandi live across the street from us. They had moved to town from their farm Prinsloo, a year before. Dupie and Irene live right next door to us. Our barbeque areas are adjacent and we climb over the low fence to each other all the time. A little way down Union Street Kerry and Kevin McCaughy live in their beautiful home. Kevin is a pharmacist and a very entertaining character with a beer in his hand.

Erica, Dirk and Gerhard, Dupie and Irene's children, were more or less the same ages as our children. They became great friends and we soon felt like family. Dupie and Clinton dreaded the time when Dirk and Michael would start with typical teenager behaviour. They are both good-looking boys with too much energy and with too many clever ideas.

Within a very short space of time we had made wonderful new friends and we felt like we belonged here. We had come home.

The nature of Clinton's work required a lot of travelling. He had to see farmers all over the Karoo. This served him well when he eventually decided to start his own irrigation business again.

Rice Irrigation Engineering CC was formed. Clinton and I were the only two employees to start off the business. We worked from home where I did the books and general office work. Because most farmers knew him and had dealt with the old Rice Irrigation from Cradock days, it did not take him long to build up this business. Clinton realized that drip irrigation was the way to go in this part of South Africa where water was scarce and precious. Drip irrigation minimizes evaporation and unnecessary loss of water and a farmer can irrigate much more land with the same amount of water. However, this concept was new and needed to be marketed well. People generally stick to familiar practices and Clinton worked hard to prove the worth of this new way of irrigation.

Tim Murray from Graaff-Reinet and Boytjie Henderson from Somerset were some of the first farmers to install drip irrigation. Their yields had increased dramatically while their water consumption had decreased considerably. Clinton took many other farmers to have a look at these pastures and the concept of drip irrigation became attractive to progressively thinking farmers. Clinton believed in solving a problem for a farmer when he sold him something. He knew that was the only way to build up a solid base of loyal clients.

At home we entered the new era of adolescent development. Gisèle had been the proverbial good girl all her life. She was sixteen now and the extremely social crowd at school invited her to every party in town. Clinton had his hands full and laid down strict curfews and laws concerning her socializing. The young admirers were petrified of him, until they got to know him better, and they became even more wary of this fiercely protective father.

Castlemaine is built with cellars underneath the lounge, dining room and kitchen. Gisèle was given permission to use one of these cellars as an entertainment area where the young crowd could get together. This dungeon was cleaned out and sparsely furnished with old chairs and a foam sofa previously used as a seat in the canopy of the old Ford. Lighting was installed as there were no windows and her friends came over to help decorate The Den. She asked if they could have carte blanche with the interior décor. I agreed, as no one else would ever go there except the youngsters, and on condition that it would not cost me any money. After some hard work she called us to have a look at the final product. Our eyes widened at the sight of spray painted graffiti on the walls and supporting pillars. Everyone that had helped with the décor, had sprayed their names somewhere or wrote something funny. The children thought it looked so cool. We thought it resembled a dark, dangerous ally in some back street and were just grateful we would not be welcome there.

That following weekend The Den was officially declared the party place. We had been invited out, but Clinton for once in his life declined a social invitation, and thought he would rather be closer to the action at home. I was amused, but quite happy to stay home to watch his reaction.

The noise from downstairs was quite deafening, but we had expected that. The smoke, though, twirling up through the two little doorstopper holes in the floorboards in our dining room caught Clinton's attention.

"What the heck! These kids are smoking down there! If you smoke you can poke!" he announced dramatically. I burst out laughing.

"My darling, did you smoke at school?" I asked innocently.

"Not during rugby season!" he replied, somewhat irritated.

After another hour or so I could see him becoming pretty worked up. I suggested that he should go down to chat to the kids. He didn't want to be a spoilsport, but thought he'd simple say hi so that they knew he was around.

Three minutes after he had gone down, there was total silence in The Den. The next moment he came back looking like an enraged lion. Apparently there was this one inebriated boy with a cigarette in his hand, who had no idea who Clinton was. He thought Clinton had come in from the street to join the party and asked him what he was doing there.

"This is my house, you little snotkop! Who the hell are you and who are your parents and where do they live?" Clinton demanded.

Gisèle's face went pale at the sound of her father's angry voice. The rest of the crowd left in a hurry, only to line up behind Gisèle five minutes later in the kitchen to apologize for the behaviour of the other boy, who had gate-crashed the party anyway.

Clinton was still fuming, but appreciated this gesture. All was forgiven, but the party had died a quiet death.

After that there were still parties in the den, but the children's behaviour was acceptable. It was quiet amusing to see all the partygoers filing into the lounge to greet Clinton first before they went down to The Den.

Gisèle and Michael kept to the curfew and arrived home at twelve on the dot one Saturday evening. They said goodnight and went to bed. I remembered something I had to ask her and popped into her room. I was surprised to see her in bed already, fast asleep at five past twelve. I called. No answer. I touched her lightly and felt the stuffing in her bed that was supposed to look like her sleeping. The window stood wide open. I went back to bed, not sure if I should say anything and hoping Clinton had dropped off to sleep. I knew Gisèle's friends and considered this a harmless bit of naughtiness.

"What's happening?" Clinton was still awake.

"Nothing really. I think she has slipped out and will be back soon." I tried to sound casual.

The next instant he was in her room. "What do you mean you *think* she has slipped out! Of course she did!" He checked Michael's room and there he was, sleeping innocently for a change.

After another hour she was still not back and Clinton's anger had turned to concern.

We had no idea where to go looking for her, so all we could do was wait. Clinton locked the window and came to bed. He bent his head in prayer and asked the Lord to protect her from all harm. He prayed for longer than I could remember. I lay in his arms and reminded him to trust in God's ability to answer his prayers. Eventually we fell asleep, only to wake every hour to check if she had come back safely. Clinton heard someone throwing small stones at Michael's window and was up like a shot. Gisèle was trying to get Michael to open the window for her and got the surprise of her life when she saw her father's face instead.

Clinton never said an angry word. He simply opened the kitchen door for her to come in. The next morning he had a calm talk with her. She had gone with all her friends to another friend's house a block away where they had played pool. She felt very guilty when she realized how worried we had been and promised not to do that again. That, however, was not enough to save her from being grounded for the term.

After a month and a half of perfect behaviour, Clinton allowed her to receive visitors at home. She knew better than to push for more than that.

Janine was very happy at school and became a member of the famous seven. These little girls did everything together and were very aware of their status as the popular group. The famous seven became the famous six after one girl left the school. Janine and René Bekker became really close friends, but had to manage their friendship carefully to prevent disruptions to the equilibrium in the group. Pre-adolescent social behaviour can be extremely complicated.

Swimming and gymnastics were Janine's best sports at junior school level. She earned provincial colours for both. She was also the victrix ludorum at the regional provincial championships gala. In gymnastics she earned provincial honours in tumbling, double mini tramp, trampoline and artistic gymnastics. She was always busy practising some or other sport, but she simply loved it here in our new environment.

Fort Street suffered a sad loss when Thandi, Sally's husband, suddenly died of a heart attack. Thandi was such a wonderful man who did not have an enemy in the world. We all missed him terribly and rallied around Sally to offer support and care. She is a strong woman who bravely faced the future without her husband. Her children, Molly-Ann and Bruce, loved and supported her every step on her road to recovery. I realized afresh the value of family unity and support in times of tragedy.

At the beginning of the Christmas holidays, a tragic accident happened to one of Gisèle's school friends. Piet Marais and his buddies were swimming in the river on their farm outside Somerset East when he dived into the river and hit a sand bank. He was paralyzed from the neck down. After months in hospital he came home in a wheelchair. His schoolmates were amazing with him. They treated him like nothing had changed. He had been a first team rugby player and his friends adored their mischievous mate.

Because she was only seventeen when she wrote her finals and did not really have a clue what she wanted to study at university, Gisèle had decided to do a post matric at Gill College. Piet and Gisèle both had many free periods a day and the two of them would often arrive at our home for a snack and drink during school time. She would push him uphill and arrive huffing and puffing after she had managed to get him up the stairs and into the lounge. On their way back she would support herself on the wheelchair's handlebars, lean forward on him and the two of them would freewheel down the steep Fort Street at horrifying speeds. College Road meets Fort Street at a T-junction and here she would put down her one foot slightly to get them to turn left. They had perfected this technique and made it look quite easy.

Into Africa

Zanny le Roux, Piet's loyal friend and aid, decided that, if she could do it, so could he. Zanny forgot to take into account that he was twice as tall and heavy as Gisèle. He pushed Piet down Union Street to his house one day and tried the same stunt. Union Street has a very long downhill and by the time Zanny put his foot out to slow them down, the whole contraption lost balance and both Piet and Zanny were flung through the air and landed in the road. Piet's wheelchair went one way he went the other. They both got the fright of their lives, but no serious injuries were sustained. Piet's mom, Marina, a wonderful teacher and mentor at Gill College, as well as the most devoted mother, just wanted to know if the wheelchair was all right. She said Piet's scratches would heal by themselves, but she didn't want to spend money on another wheelchair! Marina's sense of humour is a good indication of her wisdom and very sharp mind. After this incident Piet was discouraged from using his wheelchair as a go-cart. We all admire her for her courage and the incredible way she has with people.

Gisèle was elected first team hockey captain and received full colours for swimming, something only a few swimmers were able to attain in the past decade at Gill College. Colours were only given if you could swim a certain time at an official gala twice. Janine was the first standard six to make the first hockey team. It was a special time for them to play side by side for a season.

Michael, apart from getting into enough trouble in the boarding house, was doing very well as a hurdler and came in second at the EP championships. He also received a silver medal for gymnastics in the tumbling discipline at the South African championships in Pretoria. I was always sad that he did not continue with swimming in high school, but he had to choose one summer and one winter sport. He did qualify as a lifesaver in the surf, though.

Rugby was always his big love. Luke Watson was the first team rugby captain when Mike was in standard six, now called grade eight. The first team rugby manne (men) were hero worshipped by the younger boys. Michael was chosen for the U14 B side at center where he also did most of the kicking for poles. He played on the wing and center during his first four years at Grey and was moved to prop in his final year when he played for the first rugby team.

My sister used to say every parent thinks his crow is a peacock. Clinton watched every rugby game on a Saturday from the U 14 E's to the first team. He had a good idea of the talent around and was often frustrated at team choices, but realized there was no greater irritation for a school coach than interfering parents. He encouraged Michael to work harder and play himself into a top team. I knew very little about the rules of rugby and kept asking Clinton why the referee had blown the whistle. These constant questions and his patient answers gave me some understanding of the game. Having coached hockey for very long, I was interested in the technical side of the game. I wanted to understand the backline moves as well as the struggle up front.

When Michael was chosen for the first team in 2005 at loosehead prop, a position he had never played before, we were both surprised and excited. His friend and flyhalf, Matthew Tayler-Smith, told me that my son had become very strong and that he was doing great for the team. Matthew, or Sif, as the boys called him, and Michael are still close friends and were fellow boarders for five years.

Watching rugby at Grey is an experience one cannot describe. Home games are attended by thousands of parents, supporters and the entire school. The atmosphere next to the field can be compared to a test match. The first team always played last, at about three in the afternoon. In the stands the whole Grey student body would sing and cheer their team to victory.

We loved watching him play and tried not to miss a game. Clinton was so proud of his son who had become as strong as an ox. At this stage Michael was a lot taller than his dad. Whenever

Into Africa

he scrummed, I found myself pushing harder in the stands and praying even harder. He always scrummed his opposition to pulp. I thought he was absolutely magnificent and would have made him man of the match in every game. Our peacock was growing into a future star rugby player.

Michael was aware of his mother's bias and often reminded me that he was only doing what was expected of him. I think he dreaded the thought of me turning into one of those lunatic moms next to the field. I made sure my conduct was ladylike and composed so that he could get on with the game without having to worry about his mother behaving like a crazy fan.

Their game against Paul Roos Gymnasium, a top rugby school from Stellenbosch, was played in pouring rain on a field that resembled a pool of mud. It had been raining non-stop in Port Elizabeth for days, but no rugby game was ever cancelled due to foul weather. The Philip field had taken a beating from the games played on it since eight that morning. After ten minutes all the players looked the same – brown and soaked. Five minutes before the end the score was still equal and there was a scrum on the centre line. Gripping was impossible in the mud and the whole scrum collapsed. Suddenly I saw the physiotherapist and doctor running towards a player lying still on the field. My heart nearly stopped when I saw Michael being supported off the field. The crowd gave him a standing ovation as he was gently put down on the side with Vanda and Paul Wannenberg attending to his knee.

He was lying in great pain in the pouring rain. I prayed like crazy for him, but harder for restraint for myself not to charge down to help. After they had done what they could, there was another injury on the field and he was left to himself. I looked at Clinton and he nodded. I went down to my injured child and held the umbrella over him. He saw me and pretended to be fine all of a sudden. A mommy kneeling beside a first team rugga bugga was not part of the image. I asked him if I could pray for him and he immediately relaxed and welcomed this. I could see he was in great pain. Vanda, the physiotherapist, joined me in prayer. He had hurt his ligaments badly and she knew this was bad news before the first team tour to Argentina in six weeks time.

Clinton and I were set to join the two-week tour to Argentina during the winter holidays. Michael's knee had recovered sufficiently for him to be able to play again on tour. This was going to be quite costly, but Clinton said we would eat pap and derms (intestines and porridge) to save money. He was not going to miss this tour for anything!

We had a fantastic time in Buenos Aires, apart from the fact that we could not understand Spanish and the Argentine people could not understand English. Ordering our first meal in a restaurant was hilarious. We moo-ed like cows to indicate the type of meat we wanted, then we pointed to our buttocks to show we wanted rump steak. We eyed every plate of food carried by a waiter and would point to something on the plate we wanted to order. It was all most amusing and we laughed at one another's food that did not quite fit the order, as we meant it.

We never saw an overweight woman in Argentina. Clinton said that was because meat was so cheap in this country and people ate more protein than carbohydrates. Some of the boys were walking behind a woman with a beautiful body for a couple of blocks in the streets of Buenos Aires. When they passed her, they checked to see if her face was as stunning as her body. They could not believe it when they saw she was an old lady!

It did not take the boys long to discover where to buy the juiciest steaks for the best price. They also enjoyed the nightlife where clubs opened at 23h00 and closed at 06h00. Many of the Argentine school children would simply go to school straight afterwards. Our boys didn't see much of Argentina on our long bus trips between cities, as they needed to catch up on some sleep. We never heard half the stories about their social interaction with the pretty girls from Argentina. The evidence that they were in high demand only became obvious when we waiting in the foyer of the hotel for the bus to take us to the airport to fly back to South Africa. Scores of young ladies came to say good-bye to the boys, who were slightly embarrassed about all the attention in front of the teachers and parents.

From Buenos Aires we went on to Mar Del Plata and then south to Bahia Blanca. The boys had a blast socially and also won all their games. I think the members of staff who accompanied the group had a wonderful time, but were happy to have the responsibility of looking after a group of hot-blooded boys off their shoulders when we set foot on home ground again.

Back in Somerset business was booming. Clinton had employed two more designers to help keep up with the demand for irrigation systems. I felt we were growing a little too fast, but Clinton was so determined to expand and build up this business, that nothing could stop him. He was a turnover machine and simply loved seeing green pastures springing up like mushrooms in the dry Karoo. His passion for irrigation was inspiring to Gisèle, who decided to do a B.Sc. Degree in Agriculture at the University of the Free State. She was looking forward to working side by side with her father one day.

Somerset East is a small town with the farming community at the core of its financial stability. Many of the school children live on farms and my children were often invited to spend time with their friends on their farms. My children loved riding horse, but horses didn't seem to be too taken with them. Gisèle had broken her wrist falling off a horse years before, and Janine did her own bit of dust-eating one day on a friend's farm. At ten in the morning she left for a farm with a whole group of friends. At eleven thirty I received a call that had me shaking like a leaf. René was hysterical when she told me Janine had been thrown off a horse and was lying unconscious on a bed in the farmhouse. I was very worried when I heard one of the boys had picked her up and carried her all the way to the house. That's one thing I knew you shouldn't do – pick up a person with a possible neck injury.

I phoned Clinton, who was out of town, and asked him to pray. I would let him know what was happening when I received further news. A lady, who also happened to be a nursing sister living on the farm next door, had seen her and phoned me to calm me down. Janine had regained consciousness after twenty minutes and could move her feet and hands. The ambulance was ready to pick her up and bring her to town. I should wait at the hospital, she said. I phoned Dr Louw and rushed down to the hospital. When the ambulance stopped, all I could see were children's heads in the back. Everyone had jumped in.

She was covered in dirt and had this strange expression on her face. Her limbs were very pale and she just lay there, not knowing where she was and what had happened. Tobie said as far he could determine, there seemed to be no neurological damage, but x-rays would have to be taken to check for other damage. Janine kept on asking where she was. Every time I would tell her she was in hospital. She then wanted to know why and I would tell her she had fallen off a horse.

"Oh."

Ten minutes later she would ask the same question. This continued until five o' clock that afternoon. I started thinking she was brain damaged, but Dr Groves told me not to worry too much. Hennie Liebenberg, our pastor came to pray for her and she smiled for the first time.

Earlier that afternoon she received more visitors, but five minutes after they had left, she could not remember that they had been there. I spoke every healing scripture I knew over her and clung to them for dear life.

I stayed in hospital with her that night. The following morning she was fine and I took her home. She could remember everything that had happened after five the previous afternoon, but to this day she can't recall anything about the fall or what had passed that day until five. Because she had sustained serious concussion, she had to be very careful not to take another knock to her head for a while.

We went water-skiing two weeks later and I told her rather not to slalom in case she should fall. I might as well have saved my breath. I could see she was as right as rain. Praise God.

Five years after this drama, Janine had another little incident. We were supposed to leave early the next morning for Port Elizabeth and I asked her and Michael not to come home too late that evening.

Janine and Francois Nolte, a school friend, decided to drive out on the dirt road to The Khaya, a lovely spot on the Little Fish River outside town where the young crown liked going. Apparently there was a kudu standing in the road and she slammed on brakes. She swerved and hit a cutting, which caused the car to flip over twice. When the car came to a halt back on its wheels, Janine was missing. Faffa, a tall chap, had managed to stay inside the car. He started searching for her, using his cell phone as a torch, and found her lying in the road about twenty meters away. She got up and there was blood everywhere. He got hold of Michael, who was still probably chatting up some girl at the Blue Crane restaurant, as well as the police. Mike took Janine straight to hospital where she was cleaned up and declared well enough to go home. Her injuries were mostly deep cuts on her buttocks and ankle. She must have landed on this part of her anatomy after being thrown out through the window. She was in tremendous shock, and hurting badly.

In the meantime, I had woken up and checked the time. Half past two in the morning! I was furious with the kids for being so late and phoned Michael. He calmly told me that they were on their way home. I heard them coming in and went back to sleep as we were to leave at six. The next moment he walked into my room and told me everything was under control and I should not worry. I just needed my sleep and told him to get to bed. He switched on my light and repeated himself. Now I thought he had had too much to drink and became angry.

He spoke carefully and calmly, "Mom, your car has been dented."

I woke up with a start. "How badly? Who was driving?"

"It's a write-off."

The next moment I stood next to my bed in absolute disbelief. He stood in front of me and stopped me from running to Janine.

"Mom, she is fine, but still in shock. You can't be angry with her right now."

When Michael was sure I was calm enough, he released me.

Janine was standing in her room with only a hospital sheet covering her. She was still trembling from shock. Michael had brought waterproof covers from the hospital for her bedding to prevent the blood from staining her sheets. Her buttocks had been cut very badly. The doctor had put dressings on each buttock and blood was still oozing from the small, deep cut in her head. I was in shock too. I put her to bed and slept beside her until the first people started arriving at seven. The car was still standing next to the road and people on their way to school had seen the wreck. They all wanted to know what had happened and came rushing to our home.

I wondered why Clinton always had to be out of town the moment I had drama. I was so grateful that she had survived this accident and didn't think about my car. Not quite then, anyway. Two years later she was sure there was still a piece of glass under the skin on her one buttock. I told her it was impossible and that the lump was just scar tissue. She phoned me later to tell me that a deeply imbedded piece of glass had slowly surfaced and had been removed by Gigi's doctor. So much for my "scar tissue" theory! I was only grateful that the scars were on her backside and not on her face.

I decided my children were in need of much more prayer from us. Their guardian angels had worked overtime. I don't know how I would ever have coped with all these trials and tribulations if I didn't have the Lord to sustain me.

Clinton was very protective of his children, especially his daughters. Gisèle was at varsity having the time of her life. She shared a flat with a good friend from school, Francois Lötter. Clinton was all right with this arrangement as he felt Francois would look out for her. Little did we know how well he would look out for her. These two fell in love six months later and got married after another four years of dating.

In June 2008 Francois came to ask for permission to marry Gisèle. I had been forewarned and tried to prepare Clinton as best I could. I knew he liked Francois, but I also knew he could be a hard nut to crack when it came to his daughters. She was only twenty-three and he still felt she was his baby girl.

After watching rugby and chatting for a while, Francois plucked up enough courage to ask Clinton for his daughter's hand in marriage. Clinton stared at him for what felt like an eternity, but was only about a minute and a half. The two of them looked each other in the eye silently. You could cut the atmosphere with a blunt knife. Eventually Clinton spoke.

"If you should ever hurt her in any way, I'll come after you, my boy."

Another pregnant silence followed.

"But I don't think you will, so I give you my blessing."

Relief flooded over his face and he thanked Clinton for the trust he had in him. He promised Clinton he would take good care of Gisèle.

"Well, we have something to celebrate. Pour us a drink!" Clinton said.

The marriage date was set for 10 January 2009. Clinton drew up a list headed "Clint's mates" and ended up with two hundred names. His idea of a good wedding was having all your friends and their children in a barn on a farm with lucerne bales covered with rugs, a sheep, pig and beast on the spit and all the women bringing salads. A live Coloured band would make the music and everyone would have a real opskop (really good time).

Gisèle's idea was quite the opposite. She wanted a classic wedding with white flowers, chandeliers and place settings. She asked Clinton to remove the names of people she did not know from his list. He was not keen, until she told him what this wedding would cost him per head. For a moment he though eloping would be a better option.

She started looking around for a hall that could accommodate two hundred and fifty people and decided on the town hall in Graaff-Reinet. The historic old Dutch Reformed Church in the center of town is just opposite the town hall with the Angel Park in between. We decided to serve cocktails in the park while the guests waited for the bridal party to finish their session with the photographer.

Into Africa

Nobody in our household, except Michael who was playing rugby professionally in the Western Province, had another moment of peace or rest until everything had been organized to the last detail. Not even a gentle reminder that the date was still a long way off, could persuade her to slow down the relentless march to perfection.

Michael had been selected to play for the Western Province U19 team in 2006. During this year he attended the Rugby Performance Center under the skilful eye of Alan Zondag. He was selected for the Western Province U 21 team in 2007 and 2008. In 2008 he also played for the Western Province Vodacom Cup side. The club he plays for is Maties, the University of Stellenbosch's first team. He lives in Stellenbosch where he is as happy as a lark, surrounded by scores of beautiful girls, great friends and some of the most beautiful wine estates in the world.

Clinton and I drove around the country to watch most of his matches. These trips were wonderful. We stayed in lovely places and really enjoyed these outings as mini holidays. These games were also televised, so we would watch the game afterwards on TV again. I loved the atmosphere in the pavilion, but could really follow the game better on TV.

Sometimes Clinton combined a rugby trip with business and I would stay home to watch the game on TV. I had become a staunch supporter of Mike's team and got to meet most of his teammates. When we watched a game at home, I would dress up in one of his Province rugby jerseys, prepare snacks and settle in front of the TV, all excited and ready to scream and shout like only a mother could. Every time his face appeared on the screen, I would cheer and think what a handsome young man he had become. I think my friends came over to watch my performance as much as Michael's.

I was also choosy about whom I would invite over to watch the game on TV with me. Anybody who talked about recipes, their own children, their maids or anything else that had nothing to do with the game on the screen, was not welcome. I wanted to miss nothing, not a single move or incident. I am eternally grateful my son could not see his mother in action. He would be wary to allow me to look after his children one day.

When Clinton and I watched alone, we would shamelessly agree that Michael would, without a doubt, become a Springbok one day. His scrumming, hands and commitment stood out like a sore thumb. Not only do we love him to bits, we are his greatest fans, too.

Our children have brought us so much joy, in spite of wrecking our cars and nerves. We have our best fun times with them. We truly enjoy one another's company, jokes and laughter. When Clinton laughed, it was impossible not to laugh with him. His laugh came from deep inside him and burst forth like a cascading waterfall, splashing happiness over all those around him.

At an auction in town where furniture and other items were sold, Clinton bought me a beautiful blackwood server. He also bought a blocked print of a Baobab tree. We did not share the same enthusiasm for this piece of art. I asked him where he intended hanging this thing.

"Above the mantelpiece in the lounge, of course."

"Oh no. You can take it to your office and hang it there!" I protested.

"You may think it's just a tree badly blocked (he didn't actually say it so nicely), but when I look at it I am reminded of the wonderful times we had in Botswana."

He put it above the fireplace. I took it off and put it on a cupboard well out of sight. He would retrieve it and I would remove it again. Today it stands proudly where he had wanted it all along. When I had to decide on the cover for my book, Gisèle nodded towards the Baobab and that was it. She burst out laughing and reminded me that Clinton would have found it very amusing. I had been so full of nonsense about it, and now it would occupy a far more prominent place than in my lounge.

On the 18 December 2007 we celebrated our silver wedding anniversary at home with about thirty friends. Gisèle and Janine were in charge of the décor and food. There were candles all over and all the furniture in the lounge had been moved out to create a dance floor where we could jive to the tunes of Rod Stewart, Johnny Cash, The Beach Boys and all our other favourites. The girls decided we would have snacks throughout the evening so that none of the festivities would be interrupted by a sit-down dinner. I did the flowers – red roses all over to symbolize our love. This would be a theme party where couples would have to dress as a team. FC and Marleen came as ducktails, Josine and Jan Troskie came as PW Botha and Elize. Clinton and I would be Anthony and Cleopatra. I thought Clinton's helmet looked dashing. He said he thought he looked like a d#@*. At once stage of the evening he wore it back to front and I just shook my head.

Gisèle had picked up costumes for all of us from a party shop in Port Elizabeth. She got Michael a pirate outfit and she, Janine and René would come as three cats. I just loved my black Cleopatra wig and made my dress myself. I called it my wedding dress and got so carried away by the whole celebration that I was considering asking Michael to bring me in through the garden gate! One look from my kids cancelled this idea.

"A little over the top, don't you think Mom!"

Whenever I was summonsed to the kitchen to help with the snacks, I would say that I was still doing alterations to my wedding dress. Eventually Gisèle stormed into my room and demanded my assistance. She looked at my home made effort and pronounced it unfit to be called a wedding dress. That was a mistake and she quickly changed her verdict when she saw I was about to unpick the entire outfit to improve the fit. She just laughed and I decided it would have to do. The whole idea was to look different, not smart.

I think God gave us this incredible love for our children so that we would not kill them. Children are necessary to keep us humble, to remind us that we are mere mortals and to embarrass us often enough so that we would not brag about them too much.

I never said a word about my idea of renewing our wedding vows to the children. Clinton said that we were married and would stay married forever till death us do part. He thought the idea of renewing one's vows to be silly. He had made his commitment twenty-five years ago and nothing had changed.

The evening was one of fun and laughter. FC proposed a toast to us, and Clinton answered by saying he was looking forward to another twenty-five years, as long as behaved myself! The next moment he presented me with the most beautiful gold watch. We opened the dance floor like two teenagers in love. At half past three the next morning we went to bed, happy, blessed and exhausted.

Janine had started studying for a B.Sc. Degree at the University of the Free State at the beginning of 2008. Gisèle was in her final year and also doing research in the lab for the Department of Agriculture at varsity. She eventually completed her degree cum laude and received the prize for the top student in soil science. Her professor wanted her to do her honours, masters and doctorate, but she was in love was going to get married.

One of the students working on his honours degree in agriculture at the same university, came from Botswana, When he heard Gisèle had lived in Botswana too, he started telling her about a man called Clinton, who had swum across a river in full flood. This story had become a legend in Botswana and he was absolutely delighted to be able to tell his friends he knew this man's daughter. Of course, the story had been exaggerated so much that it was too good to be corrected.

The Western Province U21 team was to play the Leopards at Newlands and we decided to make a weekend of it. I booked a seven-bedroom holiday villa in Geneva Drive in Camps Bay for our whole family plus René, who is like a child to us, Brem and Denise Minnaar and their son Chase, and Tjaart Potgieter. This villa overlooked the Atlantic Ocean from its high position at the foot of Lion's Head. The setting was magnificent and we were blessed with beautiful weather and stunning sunsets.

On the Saturday we watched Mike play at Newlands Rugby Stadium in Cape Town. Michael's team was cooking and beat the Leopards convincingly. We celebrated in style that evening. The following morning Esmaré's husband, Brian, woke up with a bad headache. Brian still does not know why, because he recons he took it easy on the red wine. Poor Esmaré, a dodgy driver at best, had to drive to a shop early the next morning for headache tablets.

We had such fun and laughter and felt so privileged to have had this wonderful weekend together.

CHAPTER 29
A CEDAR FALLS

Two weeks later they played the Blue Bulls U21's on a Friday evening. Clinton had to see customers in Beaufort West and Jon Koster in Bonnievale. He thought he was close enough to Cape Town to watch Mike's game.

On the Friday after the game he stayed with Gus and Gigi in Kenilworth. Early the next morning he went to see his friend, Clive van Hasselt, in Constantiaberg Medi-Clinic. Clive was fighting cancer and the prognosis was not good.

He went on to Stellenbosch where he and Michael had breakfast before he left to come home. I couldn't wait for him to get home and made sure our snacks were ready for the WP-Blue Bulls game on TV. I even had enough time for a short beauty sleep.

I had just dozed off when my phone rang. It was Michael. He sounded different.

"Mom, have you heard?" he asked carefully.

"Heard what? What's wrong Michael?" I felt dread creeping up on me.

"Dad had an accident, Mom" I could hear his voice breaking.

I felt the blood draining from my brain.

"Is he all right?"

"No" is all he could utter.

I started screaming, "No, no, no! Oh my God no!" and for a minute lost all self-control. This could not be true. It was impossible. Clinton was larger than life. He was indestructible and we were still going to enjoy our old age together and play with our grandchildren. He was the love of my life and my soul mate. My mind rejected this shocker vehemently.

When I realized my son was still on the phone, I was shocked at my lack of control. I spoke calmly and started praying for strength and grace for us all to face this tragedy. I prayed to God to strengthen us and tried to focus my stunned mind on the Lord.

Gisèle was in Port Elizabeth with her fianceé, Francois. Janine had left two hours before with the Bekkers on a short holiday to Buffels Bay. I was alone at home eagerly awaiting Clinton's homecoming.

As soon as I had put the phone down, I lost it again. My mind was playing tricks on me. I was convinced I was having a nightmare and started jumping up in the air to float and prove to myself it was only a dream. No floating! Come on, try again! This is only a dream and in dreams you could defy gravity. My feet came down hard, and I knew this devastating thing had actually happened.

My screams had the dogs running for cover. When I could scream no more, I phoned my neighbour, Irene. Just before she ran over, she phoned Dupie who was playing cricket at the school. Within minutes the news had spread like a veld fire and people came rushing over to me.

Deon and Zenobia had stopped the car when Irene phoned them, and got out. Janine and René were wondering what was going on when they saw the look of concern on their faces and their obvious distress. Janine phoned me and asked what was happening. When I told her, her little voice dissolved in tears and I felt so helpless not being able to hold and comfort her. I was just grateful that she was with people she loved and who would do all they can to calm her down.

I phoned Francois to tell Gisèle and bring her home. He was so shocked that he took a while to compose himself. She took the phone from him and simply hung up in stunned disbelief when I told her.

Sonja Deetlefs, a friend and fellow hockey coach from school, arrived with the headmaster, Steven Zietsman. They immediately offered to fetch Janine.

I walked around the house and felt so empty and alone. Many friends had arrived, but I felt distant and in a very unfamiliar place. I thought of Michael who had grabbed his clothes and was headed for the scene of the accident, thirty-five kilometers on the Beaufort West side of Laingsburg. It was a two and a half hour drive for him to Laingsburg. He was alone and I was concerned for his safety. I dreaded the sight he would face and asked Dupie to speak to the police at Laingsburg to spare him as far as possible. He knew someone had to identify Clinton, and he felt he had to face this. He wasn't going to subject his mother or sisters to this devastating ordeal.

When the girls walked in, we sobbed our hearts out while clinging onto one another. We were floating on a wave that oscillated from one extreme to the other. One moment we would recall something Clinton had said and would laugh and the next moment we were swept under again by our grief.

The hours seemed like days while we waited for Michael to arrive. Dupie, Irene and Jac Troskie, a very close friend and confidante of Clinton's, waited with us until half past twelve that evening when Michael arrived home. When I saw him, he looked a lot older than the boy I had seen two weeks before. I held him to comfort him, but he had turned into the comforter. His strong arms around me brought me immense comfort and sadness at the same time. He was so brave and tried so hard to restore tranquility to our world that had been turned upside down. Within a day Michael had changed from an easygoing, mischievous boy into a man who took on the responsibility of protecting and comforting his family. Gisèle, always the organizer and director, made sure everything at home ran smoothly. Janine quietly moved into her own space of denial.

I dreaded going to bed that night. That empty space next to me was overwhelming. I couldn't face space. I needed confinement and closeness. Janine came to sleep with me, and after tossing and turning for a while, emotional exhaustion mercifully made me pass out. I slept soundly until seven the next morning without the help of the sleeping tablet someone had put on my bedside table.

I went to my happy room, a small sunroom flowing off my bedroom, with a cup of coffee for my morning talk with the Lord. I was still numb from shock and found I had no words. In fact, I could not believe I had survived the night. I could not pray and just needed to sit at the Lord's feet like a child in desperate need of love and guidance.

I simply sat there quietly, waiting for God to make the first move. After a long time, I wondered if He was ever going to pitch. Then I closed my eyes and felt His love all around me. I just sat there, holding the warm cup against my cheek, and allowing His ministering peace to restore some degree of calmness to me. More than anything, I needed His strength to support my hurting children.

I knew that Clinton's death was not God's will. It was an accident. My God is no murderer, nor is He the author of disaster. We live by choices we make. Clinton was a brilliant driver, but always drove very fast and according to police calculations he had been sending it. I do know, beyond a shadow of a doubt, that the Lord will never take away our freedom of choice. He guides us on paths of righteousness and peace, but we still have to walk the walk ourselves. A judgment error on Clinton's part could have been the cause of the accident. Who knows? How will knowing change anything?

Whatever the reason, I know God's heart. I know that He did not cause this accident. I could, therefore, sit at His feet in complete trust and allow Him to hold me and heal my broken heart slowly, piece by piece and in time. I refuse to blame Him or falsely accuse Him. While sitting there quietly, I felt His peace descend on me like a warm blanket, slowly warming my heart and gently restoring calm to my numbed senses. I felt the Lord holding me in His loving arms and asking me to keep my focus on Him. I knew then that I would survive this and be able to sustain hope and faith for my family with His help. It was not going to be easy, but I had a Helper who would never leave me, nor forsake me.

The accident had happened just before two in the afternoon on Saturday 27 September 2008. Our lives had been altered forever, but the Lord remained our constant source of hope for the future. No other vehicle had been involved in the accident. I was sure Clinton had dozed off for a moment before the car left the road. How else could this be explained? I knew he always had a short nap between half past one and two in the afternoon and the accident had occurred during that time. The car had flipped over a couple of times down an incline before coming to a stop in a barren camp. It was hard to recognize the vehicle. It was utterly destroyed. The air bags had possibly helped during the initial impact, but had deflated again by the second or third one. For a while I considered suing Mercedes Benz for the safety belt that had snapped and caused him to be thrown out through the windscreen. He had subsequently suffered a fatal injury to the back of his head. Apparently safety belts are only guaranteed up to a speed of 80 km/h. However, I let it go, as this would not bring him back, but I still think it could save future accident victims from death if these belts could be improved.

Michael's school friend, Jacques Naudé, came up from Cape Town on the Sunday to be with us. Esmaré also came to help. The two of them made tea all day long for all the visitors and generally blessed us with their love and support. Esmaré treated me to a foot massage and manicure on the Wednesday. Her skilful hands drained all the tension from my tired body and had me sleeping like a baby for about an hour and a half that afternoon.

When the funeral letter was in the process of being printed, it was Jacques who spotted a grammatical error and pointed it out to me. Having been an English teacher, I insisted on the correction and Jacques phoned the printers. They were busy printing the first page and could rectify their mistake in time.

I wanted my children to help decide on the funeral arrangements. This would be a way of starting the healing process together and coming to terms with reality. Gisèle and Janine chose the clothes he would be dressed in. They decided on his favourite outfit – his Rice Irrigation shirt, Western Province pullover, beige chino's, and his mohair socks. We all decided to see him to say our good-byes. Lyn and Gigi would go with us.

Clinton's mom was devastated. He was her first-born and they had always shared a very close bond. Gigi came to the rescue with Michael's suit that was too tight around the shoulders. She spent all day fixing it. Lyn did the coffin spray in white and cream flowers kindly sent to us by Vincent Erasmus, a business associate of Clinton's from Port Elizabeth.

I found the peace of the Lord in the sure knowledge that Clinton was with Him, to be my source of strength and comfort. His grace kept me going. I wanted my children to see faith, not fear. How could I profess to believe that we serve a God of hope and love if I fell into despair? I couldn't be strong by myself and leaned on the Lord for every bit of courage I needed to be an example of His goodness and mercy. He never failed me. His hand kept me strong. I could cry and I did, but not like someone without hope.

We were told we could see him at the funeral parlour on Thursday afternoon at two. The funeral was to be the following day. All morning I asked the Lord to help me through this moment. I wasn't sure if this was a good idea. Should I see him, or remember him the way I knew him? My children were sure and that settled it. I thought of Amanda Rabie and what she had shared with me. She had also lost her husband in a car accident and found that seeing him had helped her tremendously at the burial. It had brought closure and helped her on the road to recovery.

Wendy Henderson was manning the phone, that never stopped ringing, and took messages of condolences from people across the country. People I hardly knew were phoning and telling us how Clinton had touched their lives, or told of some good deed he had done for them. Carlin, one of my first team hockey players, took my cell phone and wrote down all the messages for me.

For two weeks cooked meals were delivered to the house. The kindness from the people of Somerset East was humbling and I knew this place had truly become our home. People never stopped arriving to show their support and love for us.

We braced ourselves and drove down to the funeral home. Before we went in, Hennie and Hendrik, our two pastors, were waiting to pray with us. I wanted to run away and pretend this was all unreal, but I drew courage from the Lord and knew I had to be strong for my family. Clinton would have wanted me to be strong. I can do all things through Christ who strengthens me, I repeated silently. I forced myself to step into the funeral home.

I saw Clinton and I reeled. He had been hurt badly and it was quite shocking to see him like this, my Clinton, who epitomized life, fun, laughter and love. Lyn cried out. and for a moment I thought she might faint. We stood around the coffin united in our pain. We held his hand for so long that it became soft and almost warm again. I stood there and I could sense he was not there. I thought of him in heaven with God, all perfectly well and happy and felt God's love enfold us all. The unknown is what most scares us about death. The comfort that comes from knowing the truth of salvation and eternal life is what kept me on my feet.

We all have to die one day. It is just so much harder when you lose someone in the prime of his life, someone that still had so much vitality, love and zest for life, someone I still needed to love and hold me and enjoy the fruit of his labour. Gisèle insisted on spending time alone next to the coffin. I prayed for strength for her as she said good-bye. My own grief was doubled as I saw my children struggling to cope with theirs.

Michael took me for a spin in the electric golf car. We went to the off-road course by the river where he drove up and down impossibly steep ramps and bush roads. The exhilaration of the drive and the fresh air in my face was wonderful. When we came back I felt a lot better. I thanked God for the incredible support my children gave me, and the little things they did to show their love and care for one another.

Before we entered the church I felt calm and composed. I was going to be all right. I could feel the strength of the Lord flowing through me. Michael stood next to me and said, "We are going to be all right, Mom. Just remember, the worst was yesterday and that is over."

The church was packed. I saw my hockey team in their school uniforms. These girls have been my joy and pride. Coaching them has been a wonderful privilege. I was humbled yet again at this show of support.

Hennie's sermon was very uplifting and he used Clinton's childlike faith as an example of how we should trust God. Rosy Hogg had made a DVD of clips from his life and these photographs were shown on the big screen next to the pulpit. A photo of Clinton sitting in the zinc tub in our khaya in Botswana brought a little laughter from the congregation and lifted the somberness for a while. The message was one of encouragement to be real with God. Clinton's relationship with God was so uncomplicated and honest. He wasn't worried about being religiously correct, as long as he was close to Him and lived in a relationship of trust and love with his Saviour.

I looked at the coffin, covered in flowers beautifully and lovingly arranged by Boomboo. I found it hard to believe that the body I had loved for so many years, was inside that wooden case, but I felt such peace knowing he wasn't really there at all. I knew where he was and that I would see him again one day. I felt the Lord's gentle love all around and all fear left me. Clinton had just got there first, to the ultimate destination where we all wanted to be.

Outside the church, the support of the people was amazing. I was so touched to see Neil Crawford, the headmaster of Grey, Jerome Paarwater, Michael's Western Province rugby coach, and so many other friends that had driven great distances to show how much they cared. I would remember every face and their presence brought me much comfort in the months that followed.

Michael had to leave on the Sunday to prepare for the semi-final Currie Cup game against the Free State the following Saturday in Bloemfontein. I received a letter from the Western Province Rugby Union executive stating that they had decided to dedicate the semi-finals to Clinton's memory. Clinton had been to every game and had a close relationship with many of the players. This honour brought tears to my eyes and I couldn't help thinking of how wonderful the WP rugby family had been to Michael.

Michael led the team onto the field and I noticed all the players had taped black bands around their left sleeves. The teams were grouped apart for a minute's silence. In the crowd Charl and Marianne Weideman sat next to us for moral support. Gisèle, Janine and René sat close to me and we all cheered loudly for the WP team and on Clinton's behalf. Michael played his heart out and so did the rest of the team. They were in the lead, but in the final seconds of the game the Free State center intercepted a dicey pass and scored. The team was so disappointed as they had had a fantastic season and were looking forward to be crowned Currie Cup Champions for the second year in a row.

We were concerned about Janine, who seemed to have withdrawn into her own world. She had no hysterical outbreaks, no breakdowns and appeared calm to the untrained eye. I sense that she is having great difficulty in dealing with Clinton's death. We are all hurting and trying our best, but her silence was too loud to be ignored.

Apart from loving her and praying for her, I don't know how else to ease her pain. It hurts me to see my children hurting. I rely on God for strength and calmness for myself so that I would be an encouragement and not a liability emotionally and spiritually to my children. I lift her in my prayers to His throne of Mercy and simply trust that she will allow Him to put her broken heart together again. She has always had a very strong relationship with Jesus and I know it will take time, but that she will heal eventually.

I often wonder what is really happening inside Michael's heart. Does he ever allow himself to just cry and let out the pain? With us he is the pillar of strength and always positive and encouraging.

He always holds us close and assures us that he is fine. His only concern seems to be for us. He is so young and I don't want my pain to burden him even more.

Michael had to undergo knee surgery after his last match. He had been playing with a loose kneecap for a while and Dr Spike Erasmus cut out a piece of his hamstring to fabricate a new ligament for his knee. The operation was a success, but the knee would require a couple of months' rest to heal properly. Michael was included in the Super 14 Stormers end-of-the-year training squad and was bitterly disappointed to miss this opportunity to train with them.

Clinton had been a constant source of inspiration to him and I pray that Mike will heal physically and emotionally enough to take on the challenge and run the race as we know he can. He has always shown enough guts when faced with a challenge, and I believe that his trust in the Lord will be his source of strength. Being a woman and his devoted mother, disqualifies me from being his objective soundboard as far as his rugby is concerned. I am often reminded that I am not his technical advisor. I can only encourage and support, and trust in the Lord for His protection and blessing for my son. I believe that Michael has what it takes to become one of the best rugby players. He will have to do the hard work himself, stay humble and never give up. Most important is the fact that all the glory belongs to the Lord and I think he knows that.

Gisèle had to step into the business and was thrown in at the deep side. Clinton *was* Rice Irrigation and it was impossible to simply take over from where he had left off. I appointed Jaco Nel as manager. Gisèle was living in Port Elizabeth and came through three or four days in the week, depending on where she was working with clients. Jaco was going through his own pain. His brother had been killed in a plane crash a couple of days after Clinton's accident.

I found it so hard to go down to the office for our management meetings. This is the place where he had built up a very successful business and his absence there was too painful for me. I tried to think what he would have done in certain circumstances, but realized no one could replace his presence there. I also knew that today's challenges could not always be solved by yesterday's solutions. I marveled at Clinton's ability to bring in business and knew he had done the work of six people. We were up for a huge challenge.

I went home and put Clinton's Baobab print up on the mantelpiece where it belongs. Whenever I look at it now, I see a man who loved life and adventure, who cared very deeply for his family, who lived a hundred years in the time span of fifty six, the love of my life, a man amongst men.

Oh God, please help and guide us in our fight for survival, I prayed. At the same time I realized He has already given us all we need to be victorious. We must simply believe that, apply His principles, and get wise strategy for every situation we would face in the business as well as emotionally.

CHAPTER 30
THE WEDDING

All the firsts were going to be hard, I knew. Gigi and Gus had invited us to spend Christmas with them at Bushmans. We had a wonderful time water skiing and relaxing at their rented home which overlooked the river. When Kate arrived she brought more laughter and fun and we all had a super holiday. I water-skied for the first time in many tears and thought of how Clinton would have encouraged me and how he would have so proud of his old goose.

Gisèle and Francois' wedding was set for 10 January 2009. We went home to prepare for the final stretch.

The entire Karoopark Guest House in Graaf-Reinet was booked by the family. In fact, the wedding guests had booked up all the Camdeboo Cottages as well. Buks and Louise Marais and their daughters Chantel and Marizaan made sure we were spoiled rotten. On the Friday we celebrated Francois' birthday and the party continued till the early hours of the morning. Buks had organized a sunset game drive for the men who were more interested in the cold box with the booze than the beautiful animals around them. Friday evening was a happy family re-union where we all shared our news and everybody renewed bonds of friendship. Clinton's absence was almost too hard for me to bear, and I went to bed before midnight.

My mom had baked and decorated the wedding cake. It was a masterpiece of old world charm and classic elegance all in white. Of course, the cake was a real fruitcake made with homemade fruit preserve. It weighed a ton!

Louise put me in the honeymoon suite where Clinton and I had slept before. This room was to be the place where the bride would get dressed as well. Gisèle and her three bridesmaids, Janine, Esmaré and Tanja were sharing a suite. René shared the room with me and made sure everything I needed was right there.

The day of the wedding arrived. I had been doing all the flowers the previous day as well as on the Saturday morning. At four o' clock that afternoon we were all dressed and ready. Lyn had done all the bouquets, buttonholes, and corsages with Gigi as her assistant. They had been absolutely incredible in their support emotionally and practically.

" Jacques, Cecile and Michael"

"Francois, Gisèle, Michael, Cecile and Janine"

Gisèle looked incredibly beautiful as Michael brought her down the aisle. I couldn't help thinking of how proud Clinton would have been at her side. I prayed that we would be able to control our emotions and make her day one of happy memories. Jacques had taken me into the church and I sat between him and Michael. My heart was beating like crazy and I started shaking. Mike put his arm around me to steady me. Her handsome husband-to-be looked at her with adoration and pride as she stood next to him in front of the imposing pulpit of the Groot Kerk where Hennie was ready to start the ceremony. The bridesmaids and groomsmen looked so good and completed the picture Gisèle had always dreamed of.

During Francois' powerful speech at the reception he nearly had us all in tears when he spoke to Clinton and said, "Uncle Clinton, I mean Dad,… I will not break my promise to you."

Janine never stopped dancing. At one stage she nearly twirled out of her dress. Michael was the perfect pillar of strength and so attentive and protective. The rest of the evening flew past in record time. It had been the most beautiful wedding and everybody had had a fantastic time. The last guests left at five in the morning.

On our way back to Somerset, Janine and I reflected with gratitude on what a success the wedding had been. Our feet were killing us from all the dancing and work and we were bone tired. I felt flat for the first time in months. I missed Clinton. I needed him. It felt so wrong that he had not been part of the wedding. I started focusing on my loss and of course, it didn't take much to start the tears flowing.

At home I went into the garden and sobbed. I cried until I felt weak. Suddenly I heard a voice deep inside me telling me to stop and think. What was I doing? I had a choice here and I had chosen to be ungrateful, pathetic, weak and full of self-pity, instead of thankful for a wonderful wedding, many friends and incredible children. I started counting my blessings and thanked God every one I could think of. The change in my mood was incredible.

Depression and hurt slowly started giving way to peace, joy and hope. I asked the Lord to hold me and never let me go, to forgive me for focusing on negative thoughts and sadness instead of on His loving kindness.

I have learnt that in order to be kind to myself, I have to be hard on myself. I have to recognize fear, self-pity and depression when they rear their ugly heads to steal my joy and shift my focus away from God. Stress is a kind word for fear, and fear is the opposite of faith. Without faith it is impossible to please God, and life is only worth living when I am in a very close relationship with Jesus. He loves me. He is for me and not against me. He will be my protector, my guide, my reason for living a life that will bless my children and all those around me.

I know I will fail at times, but I will get up and face my choices again.

Today I choose Life, Peace, Joy, Hope, Courage, Strength, Protection, Provision and all else I find in Him and through Him.

Nothing more.

Nothing less.

CPSIA information can be obtained at www.ICGtesting.com
Printed in the USA
LVOW081713240512
283169LV00006B/2/P